THE ARTS IN BRITAIN
IN WORLD WAR I

THE ARTS IN BRITAIN
IN WORLD WAR I

JOHN FERGUSON

President, Selly Oak Colleges, Birmingham
Formerly Dean and Director of Studies in Arts
The Open University

Typeset by Malvern Typesetting Services
Printed in Great Britain at The Camelot Press Southampton

Ferguson, John, *b. 1921*
   Arts and society in Britain during World War One.
   1. Arts, Modern—20th century—Great Britain
   2. Arts and society—Great Britain
   3. European War, 1914-1918—Art and the war
   I. Title
   700'.941   NX543

ISBN 0-85249-548-X

709.42

FOR KEN AND HELEN

Contents

Illustrations

Acknowledgments

Ben Uri Art Gallery 1; The Elgar Foundation 28; Fitzwilliam Museum, Cambridge 33; Imperial War Museum, 4, 5, 6, 7, 8, 9, 10, 11, 12, 14, 15, 23, 25, 26, 27, 41, 43, 44, 45, 46, 47, 48, 49, 50; International Museum of Photography 24; Kettle's Yard, University of Cambridge 31; King's College Library, Cambridge 53; National Portrait Gallery 3, 29, 30, 32, 34, 35, 36, 38, 39; Punch 52; Royal College of Music 40; Tate Gallery 2, 13, 16, 17, 18, 19, 20, 21, 22, 37, 42; University Library, Cambridge 51.

Introduction

THE Open University has tried in its teaching to break down the
barriers between traditional departments, disciplines and subjects of
study. It was therefore a particular thrill to be invited to serve on the
editorial committee for this new series, and to contribute one of the
first volumes, taking up and expanding some work I had done for the
Open University course on *War and Society*.

The work was not easy to organize, and I am not wholly satisfied
with my solution. It seemed best to make a broadly chronological
analysis; we can indeed recognize three broad periods: the outbreak,
the central period of digging in and the final months of bitterness.
But it was not possible to be strictly chronological; moods
overlapped, and one logic conflicted with another. To take one small
example. In 1917 Kipling published a volume of short stories, mostly
written before the war, but including two written during the war's
early stages; where can this be appropriately discussed? In particular,
11 November 1918 was not a date at which a rigid dividing-line
could be drawn.

I have repeated some few phrases which I used in the introduction
to *War and the Creative Arts* (Macmillan and Open University Press,
1972), and *War, The Arts, and Ideas* (Open University Press, 1973).
No one could pretend to be expert in all that I treat here. Inevitably I
have sometimes relied on the opinions of others, though I have done
my best to make them my own, and have thought about all the works
I treat. In recent years there have been a number of perceptive
treatments of the literature, by Bergonzi, Johnston, Silkin and
others. Something comparable about the art is much to be desired. I
must pay tribute here to one book from which I have learned a lot
and pillaged shamelessly. This is E. D. Mackerness's *A Social History*

of English Music (Routledge and Kegan Paul, 1964). The eleven pages 236–46 are sheer gold, and the whole book an outstanding example of social history applied to the arts. I have submitted a draft of the work to my colleagues Trevor Bray, Charlotte Benton, Nick Furbank and Arthur Marwick, and am grateful for their expert criticism. I fear that I have sometimes retained my own value-judgements against their advice. I am grateful to Trevor Bray for information about Havergal Brian's letters. Thanks to my fellow-editors, especially Allen Percival, and to the staff of Stainer and Bell, and especially Gwenllian Rhys, for their help and encouragement. Thanks also to Elron Press for undertaking the editorial work. I am grateful to Peggy Mackay for undertaking the typing even before meeting me. And my wife has once again contributed one of her impeccable indexes.

1

The Shaking of the Foundations

W HEN Queen Victoria died on 22nd January 1901, it seemed as though an epoch had ended. She had been on the throne for nearly two-thirds of a century. It was an era in which the Union Jack was raised in the empire on which the sun never set; an era in which ordered government had been established, backed by respectable religion; an era of educational expansion; the era of the Great Exhibition and the Albert Hall; the era when performances of Handel's *Messiah* (in massive un-Handelian pomposity), Mendelssohn's *Elijah* and Stainer's *Crucifixion* became almost rituals; the era of imperialism and social reform. The Royal Academy was enormously prestigious; the Grosvenor Gallery from 1877 onwards began to offer more refreshing exhibitions. The New English Art Club was formed in 1885, and offered a fresh impulse to contemporary artists. The National Gallery was extended in 1887; the City of London Corporation Gallery, the Whitworth Institute in Manchester and the Irish Art Museum in Dublin were all opened in 1890; the National Portrait Gallery opened in 1896, the National Gallery of British Art (The 'Tate') in 1897, and the Wallace Collection in 1900. In music, Sterndale Bennett did important work at the Royal Academy of Music, and the foundation of the Guildhall School in 1880 and the Royal College in 1883, and the opening of the Queen's Hall in 1894, gave promise for the future. There was hope that the new century would bring new progress.

Although they did not realize or recognize it at the time, the British were pioneers in at least one branch of the arts—and that was architecture. The Glasgow School of Art (1896), designed by Charles Rennie Mackintosh (1868–1928) is now viewed as one of the seminal buildings of modern architecture, honest and straightforward,

1

deriving from a sensitive regard for the materials used and an awareness of basic function. Even the ornaments are not superfluous but arise from a functional need and express the nature of the materials used. The other outstanding architect and designer of the time was Charles Annesley Voysey (1857–1941), whose strength lay in his sense of form. His own house, 'The Orchard' at Chorleywood (1900) is composed asymmetrically of simple forms. All the elements are clear and defined; overcrowded decoration is totally eliminated and the forms speak for themselves. Mackintosh was, however, to withdraw into alcoholic addiction, and had no real successor, and Voysey's designs were copied by architects who lacked his sense of style and expressed a superficial similarity without any deep purpose of form or function. Suburban and garden-city building followed Voysey—but a long way behind. How little effect they had on development in Britain is seen by the fact that the first really modern house in Britain was built by a German architect, Peter Behrens, for the Bassett-Lowkes in Northampton as late as 1926.

Writing in 1915, the editor of *The Connoisseur* could also declare that in engraving, domestic architecture, and the production of furniture and ceramics Britain led the world at the outbreak of war. This is dubious, although it is right to remember the work of Sir Arthur Liberty (1843–1917) and Sir Ambrose Heal (1872–1959). Liberty was the older man; he had been a friend of Rossetti and Morris, Burne-Jones and Whistler. In his youth he had become involved in trade with the East, and he called his first independent business premises East India House. As early as 1875 he realized the potential of oriental design for textiles, and developed high-quality fabrics and fine dyes. Heal's father was a furniture dealer, he was apprenticed to the trade and became a true craftsman with a real appreciation of wood. Influenced by Voysey and others, he turned against fussiness of design and looked for functional simplicity. His salesmen had difficulty in selling this 'prison furniture', but when he won a design prize at Paris in 1900 for a bedroom suite his patronage grew. During the war he helped to found the Design and Industrial Association, and was amongst those who changed the taste of a generation. Liberty's held to a Tudor image, but Heal right at the end of the war was insisting that the best economy was solid, functional furniture. His firm has retained their reputation for craftsmanship.

2

But there were cracks in the fabric. R. C. K. Ensor put it well: 'The sky of England had been clouding for years before; what with the collapse of the country-side, the new-born social unrest in the towns, the waning of religious faith, and above all the sense of uncontrollable transition to the unknown—the feeling that the keys of power were blindly but swiftly transferring themselves to new classes, new types of men, new nations. The Queen's death focused it all.'

During the reign of Edward VII and the early years of George V, some constructive and forward-looking acts were passed, Balfour's Education Act and Lloyd George's National Insurance Act among them; and Campbell-Bannerman left his mark on the future by turning the Colonies into Dominions. In retrospect, however, these years seem only an interlude before the catastrophe of 1914. Disaster was sweeping inexorably forward. When the war came it seemed—at least for those in power—as though an era of massive and secure optimism had ended. This was true not only in Britain, but also in most of Europe. The war was the culmination, not the cause, of the breakdown of the old world.

As is often the case, those of artistic sensitivity seem to have had an intuition of what was happening and reflected it in their work before the final explosion. The early years of the twentieth century saw more radical disorientation than produced by the Impressionists in the previous generation.

Picasso's *Les Demoiselles d'Avignon* expresses something of the new forces. The Cubists, the Fauves, the Expressionists, the Futurists were all, in their different ways, in reaction against the old order. Similarly in music, Debussy had loosened traditional structures, and opened the way to the more strident and startling innovations of Stravinsky and Schoenberg. Britain, conspicuously lacking in creative genius at that period, lagged behind in both fields, though the New English Art Club had at least caught up with the Impressionist vision.

English literature had been a world force in the nineteenth century but Tennyson had been succeeded as Poet Laureate by Alfred Austin, a versifier now only remembered for his unhappiest lines. He was followed by Robert Bridges, an impeccable and skilled craftsman on a minor scale. Although Baudelaire had thrown some grey shadows on English letters, the creative poets of the early century, Rilke and Stefan George and Blok, had hardly touched England. Two giants.

3

Meredith and Swinburne, had died in 1909, but Hardy lived on, now over seventy. Wells, Bennett and Galsworthy seemed dwarfed by the shadows of Dickens, George Eliot and the Brontes. Conrad, the best of the novelists, was not even English and his finest work lay behind him. The volcano that was D. H. Lawrence was only beginning to erupt. A pall of intolerable complacency polluted the air.

Eddie Marsh fostered his smoothly unexciting volumes of *Georgian Poetry*. 'I liked poetry' he wrote later, 'to be . . . intelligible, musical and racey and I was happier with it if it was written on some formal principle which I could discern . . . I liked poetry that I wanted to know by heart, and could learn by heart if I had time.' It is hard to discern in these suave, urbane verses the crises to come, the imminent explosion in Ireland, the tension of rich and poor, let alone the abortive revolution in Russia, the imperialism of the Wehrmacht, or even the dramatic change the Wright brothers and Marconi were between them to bring to the scene. The war came to England as the messenger of death bursts in on the play of the courtiers in Shakespeare's *Love's Labour's Lost*.

The Irish scene by contrast was bright in 1914. Standish O'Grady (1846–1928) did more than anyone else to familiarize the educated Irish with their own inheritance. In 1899 the Irish Literary Theatre was formed to bring world drama to Ireland. Three years later, through two actors named Fay, the movement took a more nationalist turn, and first the Irish National Dramatic Company and then the Irish National Theatre Society emerged. Ironically, it was an Englishwoman, Annie Horniman, who gave it a home in the famous Abbey Theatre. AE (G. W. Russell), Lady Gregory and Yeats all contributed plays, as did that fine craftsman Edward Martyn, and the nearly-great Padraic Colum. But it was the emergence of J. M. Synge (1871–1909) as a dramatist of world stature which 'made' the Abbey Theatre. It is strange, reading the plays now, to realize that Synge was regarded as controversial. Irish purists regarded his candid depiction of human qualities as an aspersion on the purity of their women, the honesty of their men, and the integrity of their religion. As so often happens, it was the noise of his opponents which attracted the attention of others to the works criticized, and made the world aware of the Irish revival. Synge had two great gifts beyond any of his contemporaries; one was a sense of the theatre, the other the power to convey the lilting speech-rhythm of the Irish peasantry. The revival

4

was not confined to the theatre. George Moore (1852–1933), an Irish-born emigrant to Paris and London, had returned to Ireland in reaction against the Boer War, and spent the first years of the century there; the result was the exquisite evocation of Ireland in *The Untilled Field* (1903), and the mischievous picture of the Irish literary scene in *Hail and Farewell* (1911). AE (G. W. Russell 1867–1935) edited *The Irish Homestead* from 1904 to 1923. W. B. Yeats (1865–1939) was a greater and more influential figure than these. His early work is a romantic, escapist, melodious creation of the Celtic dreamland. But, as John Davidson put it, he had too much 'blood and guts' to remain in this tradition. By the end of the century he was exploring the inner life with the help of symbols drawn from Celtic mythology. By the time he published *The Green Helmet* in 1910 all cloudiness had blown away. The imagery is concrete, the language simple, the impact immediate. In 1914 he published *Responsibilities*, where the elements of contemporaneity, of involvement with the present world, and almost inevitably satire, are uppermost.

> What need you, being come to sense,
> But fumble in a greasy till
> And add the halfpence to the pence
> And prayer to shivering prayer, until
> You have dried the marrow from the bone?
> For men were born to pray and save:
> Romantic Ireland's dead and gone,
> It's with O'Leary in the grave.

(W. B. Yeats, *Collected Poems*, London 1950)

1914 also saw the publications of *Dubliners* by James Joyce (1882–1941), the pieces having been written over the previous decade or so. They are a flexing of Joyce's literary muscles for *Ulysses*; he communicates Dublin and its life swiftly and economically, in a way which won the exacting admiration of Ezra Pound. He himself wrote to his publisher of these sketches; 'My intention was to write a chapter of the moral history of my country and I chose Dublin for the scene because that city seemed to me the centre of paralysis.' The development continued in *A Portrait of the Artist as a Young Man*, which appeared in the magazine *The Egoist* in the early months of the war. The book is deeply touched by and at the same time in rebellion against Irish life and the Catholic religion, intense, proud and realistic, yet in its assertion of the validity of art for itself curiously reminiscent of the 1890s. There is a sense in which this is very much a pre-war work, just as *Ulysses* is equally clearly a postwar work.

The most formative point of the London scene in the period immediately preceding the war was the *salon* of Lady Ottoline Morrell (1873–1938), half-sister to the Duke of Portland. She was, in Lord David Cecil's words, 'Brilliant, idealistic and eccentric'. Quentin Bell called her a 'fantastic baroque flamingo'. She revolted against the traditionalism of her upbringing. In 1902 she married Philip Morrell, who entered Parliament in 1906, and she interested herself for a while in Asquith, Grey and Haldane, but politics was not her forte. From 1905 onwards their house in Bedford Square became the meeting-point for a constellation of talent. There could be found Sir Leslie Stephen's daughters Virginia (Woolf) and Vanessa (Bell), the radical philosopher Bertrand Russell, the economist Maynard Keynes, writers such as Lytton Strachey, Siegfried Sassoon, Walter de la Mare, D. H. Lawrence, and the Americans Henry James or T. S. Eliot, Irish poets such as W. B. Yeats or James Stephens, artists such as Augustus John, Walter Sickert and Henry Lamb and the critic Roger Fry. Some were lame dogs who needed helping over stiles, some were established figures, others showed brilliant promise, but all were interesting. This was the Bloomsbury group. Their hostess, in her own volatile, magnetic, sometimes quarrelsome way, was the still centre of their turning world. A pacifist herself, when war came she did much to help those like Russell, Sassoon or Strachey, who stood against it.

The Bloomsbury set showed a taste for discussion, for un-conventionality, for truth, for male-female equality, and for the use of Christian names. Virginia Woolf, who at this time was labouring through the seven years' gestation of her first novel, *The Voyage Out* (1915), said that at their best they kindled 'not that hard little electric light we call brilliance as it pops in and out upon our lips, but the more profound, subtle, and subterranean glow which is the rich yellow flame of rational intercourse.'

The revolutionary year in music is often seen as 1912–1913, the year of Schoenberg's *Pierrot Lunaire* and Stravinsky's *Le Sacre du Printemps*, although neither Schoenberg nor Stravinsky had any great impact on British music. Henry Wood, a remarkable pioneer, had actually played Schoenberg's *Five Orchestral Pieces* in 1912, and been hissed for his pains. This was the occasion of his famous injunction to the orchestra in rehearsal: 'Stick to it, gentlemen! Stick to it! This is nothing to what you'll have to play in twenty-five years' time!' Beecham, too, had played an important rôle, not merely in encouraging British composers, but in bringing some of the most important contemporary music from the Continent. His first season at Covent Garden actually contained five operas by living composers out of eight in all. One of these was Richard Strauss's *Elektra*, within a year or so of its first performance. The score, which now appears in many ways traditional, scared many professional players; the stage-violence horrified moralists; Stanford described the thing as 'pornographic rubbish'. Unfortunately Beecham's notorious tendency to redress the practice of others by letting the orchestra dominate the scene, did not do justice to the subtleties of a piece in which action and words are of more than usual significance. Shaw said that Beecham occasionally made the score sound like a concerto for six drums. However, the first night was packed out, and enthusiastically received. The box office success did not last, and the general view of the British public may be typified by a remark by George V: the Grenadier Guards Band had played a pot-pourri of music from *Elektra* at Buckingham Palace when a page came out with a note for the Bandmaster which read, 'His Majesty does not know what the Band has just played, but it is *never* to be played again.' British music, through Elgar and Delius, was again creative after the Victorian doldrums but it was scarcely *avant-garde*.

The pre-war theatre was dominated by four major dramatists. The oldest of them, A. W. Pinero (1855–1934), who with H. A. Jones (1851–1929) had revivified the English theatre, and who had made his own reputation and that of Mrs. Patrick Campbell with *The Second Mrs. Tanqueray* (1893), still dominated the 1900s, but after 1909 had virtually worked himself dry. Bernard Shaw (1856–1950) had not turned to the theatre until 1892, and for the next twelve years, though he had a reputation in the U.S.A., was a minor figure in the British theatre. It was the series of productions at the Court Theatre from 1904 to 1907 which put him on the map; they included *John Bull's Other Island, Man and Superman, Major Barbara* and *The Doctor's Dilemma*. This cleared the way for the later successes, especially *Fanny's First Play* with Lillah McCarthy (1911) and *Pygmalion* with Mrs. Patrick Campbell ('not bloody likely') and Sir Herbert Tree (1914). James Barrie (1860–1937) had turned to the theatre at about the same time as Shaw; his first real success was *Quality Street*, performed in America in 1901 and London in 1902 (with Ellaline Terriss and Seymour Hicks). Its sentimentality was not to all tastes, but its humour and ingenuity of plot gave it a run of 459 performances; curiously, it was immensely popular in Berlin during the War. This was followed by *The Admirable Crichton* (1902), with du Maurier, Irene Vanbrugh and Henry Kemble, *Peter Pan* (1904), and after some less successful offerings, *What Every Woman Knows* (1908). Over the next six years his contribution to the theatre was less significant, and it took the War to restore him to favour. John Galsworthy (1867–1933) was later in coming to the theatre, but was more immediately successful. He was fortunate in having Harley Granville-Barker to produce his first play, *The Silver Box* (1906), but the play itself is skilfully constructed, and Galsworthy is a master of varied but natural dialogue, free from the stagey language of Pinero or Jones and not needing the flashing epigrams of Wilde or Shaw. Galsworthy's plays are dominated by social concerns; in *The Silver Box* the inequality of rich and poor before the law, in *Justice* (1910) the insensitive impersonality of the legal system. These were the leading figures, but others should not be forgotten, able writers and competent craftsmen like St John Hankin, John Masefield, Granville-Barker himself. Gilbert Murray's translations of Euripides into mellifluous Swinburnian rhythm and rhyme may have drawn strictures from T. S. Eliot and others, but audiences liked them in their day, and they brought the classical plays back to the theatre.

The day of the great actor-managers was not yet past. Sir Herbert Tree (1853–1917) opened Her Majesty's Theatre in 1897, where he might be seen in Shakespeare, or dramatizations of novels by Tolstoy, Dickens, Dumas or Thackeray and in roles as varied as D'Artagnan, Bottom, Nero, Sir Peter Teazle, Beethoven and Macbeth. Frank Benson (1858–1939) dominated the scene at Stratford from 1886 to the end of the War, apart from eight major seasons in London, touring companies in Britain (sometimes three at once) and overseas (he made a notable tour of North America in 1913–1914). Benson was not an outstanding actor, though his Richard II and Petruchio are remembered, but he was outstanding in his encouragement of others and his infectious enthusiasm for Shakespeare. These were, however, essentially relics of the past but two other major figures pointed forward. One was Ellen Terry's son Gordon Craig (1872-1966). Craig had spent eight years with Irving at the Lyceum and had himself performed a notable Hamlet for Ben Greet in an emergency. Then in 1897 he suddenly gave up acting, and from the early 1900s his distinctive qualities as a designer began to emerge. He greatly simplified the customary elaborate décor, and fostered broad monumental effects of light and shade, preferring his scenes lit from above. Costumes were planned as part of a tableau, subtle in grey and brown, but with rich splashes of colour when appropriate. In 1905 he published *The Art of the Theatre*, in which he argued for a single art directed by a single mind. Max Reinhardt was his chief disciple and the word *Craigische* was added to the German language; ironically, Tree rejected Craig's designs for *Macbeth*. But W. B. Yeats believed in Craig, who was in the Abbey theatre in 1911, and in the same year a public banquet in London acknowledged his international reputation. The other creative genius was Harley Granville-Barker (1877-1947), who, in partnership with Vedrenne, the manager of the Court Theatre, in 1904-1907, and thereafter at the Savoy, brought new standards to stage direction. Barker brought to his productions four great gifts: first, a thorough knowledge of the theatre from inside; second, a complete intellectual, analytical and sympathetic mastery of a play; third, immense imaginative power, and especially understanding of human beings; and fourth, patience and good humour.

Since about 1906 Roger Fry (1866-1934) had been fascinated by contemporary French painting and by Cézanne in particular. This led to the directors of the Grafton Galleries inviting him, in 1910, to mount an exhibition of contemporary French art. The exhibition, 'Manet and the Post-Impressionists' was opened in November with Cézanne, Gauguin, Van Gogh, Picasso, Signac, Derain, Friesz and Matisse all represented. In terms of attendance the exhibition was a tremendous success, with never less than 400 people visiting the exhibition on any one day, but, for the most part, reactions varied from uncomprehending laughter to virulent hostility. One visitor is said to have laughed so loudly at Cézanne's portrait of his wife that 'he had to be taken out and walked up and down in the air for five minutes'. Wilfrid Blunt wrote in his diary:

9

15th November To the Grafton Gallery to look at what are called the Post-Impressionist pictures sent over from Paris. The exhibition is either an extremely bad joke or a swindle. I am inclined to think the latter, for there is no trace of humour in it. Still less is there a trace of sense or skill or taste, good or bad, or art or cleverness. Nothing but the gross puerility which scrawls indecencies on the walls of a privy. The drawing is on the level of that of an untaught child of seven or eight years old, the sense of colour that of a tea-tray painter, the method that of a schoolboy who wipes his fingers on a slate after spitting on them. . . . Apart from the frames, the whole collection should not be worth £5, and then only for the pleasure of making a bonfire of them. Yet two or three of our art critics have pronounced in their favour. Roger Fry, a critic of taste, has written an introduction to the catalogue, and Desmond MacCarthy acts as secretary to the show. . . . They are the works of idleness and impotent stupidity, a pornographic show.

(Wilfrid Blunt, *My Diary*, London 1919–20)

'Two or three' critics was right: apart from Fry and MacCarthy (whose introduction to the exhibition was cautiously worded), the only favourable London critic was Sir Charles Holmes. *The Times* saw in the exhibition 'the rejection of all that civilisation has done, the good with the bad'; their writer was rash enough to appeal to the verdict of Time, *'Le seul classificateur impeccable'*; it has certainly come down on the side of Roger Fry. The British public, cultivated leaders of taste or men in the street, were obviously not ready for such drastically new paintings. Roger Fry wrote 'There has been nothing like this outbreak of militant Philistinism since Whistler's day.' Undaunted, Fry, who was considered the leader of the avant-garde in England, went on to organize the second Post-Impressionist Exhibition of late 1912 which included work by Duncan Grant, Vanessa Bell, Wyndham Lewis, Spencer Gore, Frederick Etchells, Miss Etchells, Eric Gill, Adeney, Henry Lamb and Stanley Spencer. While none of the English artists could be said to be revolutionary, for the first time their own brand of post-impressionism was seen in context with the mainstream developments of modernist art in Europe.

In Italy Filippo Tommaso Marinetti had, in 1909, declared the death of Past-ism and the birth of Futurism in art. This was taken up by the painter Umberto Boccioni and others. The Futurists stood for novelty and against tradition, they believed that movement, dynamism, change was universal, and must be rendered in painting or sculpture as a dynamic sensation. Their principal point was expressed by Boccioni: 'A clean sweep should be made of all stale and threadbare subject-matter in order to express the vortex of modern life—a life of steel, fever, pride and headlong speed.' Their importance lies partly in the technique of arousing a dynamic sensation ('a galloping horse has not four legs but twenty') and partly in their exaltation of the machine ('a racing car is more beautiful than the Victory of Samothrace'). Ironically, though they glorified war as a cleansing power, agitated for Italy to join in, and celebrated war in their works, the movement was to be broken by the war, and by Boccioni's accidental death, while convalescing from war wounds. In 1912 there was a Futurist exhibition in London which Sickert described as a 'sudden explosion in Sackville Street, next door to Whistler's tailor, of this strange artistic camera, like the firework that is described in Messrs Brock's catalogue as "The-Devil-among-the-Tailors"'. Despite this whimsy, Sickert approved of Futurism, with its rejection of the hypnotism of the past for an active concern with the present, and its exaltation of courage and heroism. The following year Marinetti appeared in person. His most ardent supporter was C. R. W. Nevinson (1889–1946), who banged a big drum behind a curtain as a suitably militant accompaniment to Marinetti's declamation. Between them they drew up a manifesto in 1914 which attacked the Pre-Raphaelites, Oscar Wilde and Aestheticism, Garden Cities, the revival of Morris dancing, and the New English Art Club (which was emphatically not Futurist). It called for England to lead the world into the new age of the machine.

The *enfants terribles* of the British scene were Ezra Pound (1885–1972) and Wyndham Lewis (1882–1957) who both came from North America. Wyndham Lewis called Pound the 'impresario' of 'the men of 1914', meaning the revolutionaries. Pound was amusingly caricatured by John Felton in *The Egoist* (1 August 1914), a patchwork of derivations, Transatlantic snobbery, personal vanity, a Nonconformist conscience, a pursuer of novelties, vulgar and flashy in style, looking like a whitened golliwog on a cleft carrot. Pound was the publicist for the Imagists, who had formulated their creed in 1913 in reaction against the prevailing poetic culture:

1. To use the language of common speech, but to employ always the *exact* word, not the merely decorative word.

2. To create new rhythms as the expression of new moods. We do not

11

insist upon 'free-verse' as the only method of writing poetry. . . . We do believe that the individuality of a poet may often be better expressed in free verse than in conventional forms.

3. To allow absolute freedom in the choice of subject.

4. To present an image. We are not a school of painters, but we believe that poetry should render particulars exactly and not deal with vague generalities.

5. To produce poetry that is hard and clear, never blurred or indefinite.

6. Finally, most of us believe that concentration is the very essence of poetry.

(R. Aldington and Amy Lowell, *Some Imagist Poets*, 1913)

T. E. Hulme (1881–1917), a man who liked to appear tough and carried a brass knuckle-duster as a sex-symbol, had translated Sorel's *Reflections on Violence*. He rushed to enlist in August 1914 and wrote five little poems exemplifying the movement:

> Above the quiet dock in midnight,
> Tangled in the tall mast's corded height,
> Hangs the moon. What seemed so far away
> Is but a child's balloon, forgotten after play.

It is oriental in its economy. (It is somewhat ironical that Hulme was a member of the committee which awarded a prize to Rupert Brooke's 'Grantchester'.)

Wyndham Lewis was a striking figure. Violet Hunt recalled his 'deep, dark, Italian eyes, looking out of a fuzz of hair flanking on either side the upturned collar of an Inverness cape'. With the cape went a broad-brimmed hat and a straggly moustache, and an air which he himself compared to that of a character in some Russian novel. He was interested in Futurism and helped Nevinson to organize a dinner to welcome Marinetti, but regarded his attachment to the machine as sentimental. He set himself to find a creed which would express the insights of Futurism without its error.

In early 1914 Wyndham Lewis published the first issue of his iconoclastic *Blast*. It was just at this time that Pound thought of the term Vorticism to represent the movement for which they stood, the vortex being that 'from which, and through which and into which, ideas are constantly rushing'. Wyndham Lewis was to give Vorticism expression in paint, Ezra Pound in poetry and Henri Gaudier-Brzeska in sculpture. What Gaudier thought about his rôle is not clear. He

12

was an *émigré* from France, struggling with poverty, and just over twenty years of age. Certainly the philosophy of Vorticism was not his; he was no philosopher and preferred to go off and draw animals in the zoo. Winifred Gill gave a sensitive description of him:

> His eyes were quick and bright as an animal's
> That lives by its wits in a hedge, wide-set
> In a sallow face, and of so dark a brown
> Across these fifteen years they might be black,
> Glancing out through the strayed wisps of his hair.

There was an irony about Gaudier's end. In 1912 he deserted from the French army, refusing to return for military service. But in 1914 he said 'I'm going, I absolutely must'; he was in the front line by October and killed in the following year.

Blast had appeared on 20 June, 1914. It had all Marinetti's aggressiveness and was on a colossal scale (12" x 9½") with a lurid puce cover, shouting type, and provocative writing. It blasted the nineteenth century, the 'abysmal inexcusable middle class', the upper and lower classes. Wyndham Lewis was no respecter of person, even Pound was not exempt from his thrusts: he called Pound a revolutionary simpleton. But however tempestuous an image Lewis might choose to evoke he was carefully selective in his attitudes. For the Vorticist exhibition in March 1915 he wrote a note in the catalogue: 'By Vorticism we mean (a) ACTIVITY as opposed to the tasteful PASSIVITY of Picasso; (b) SIGNIFICANCE as opposed to the dull or anecdotal character to which the Naturalist is condemned; (c) ESSENTIAL MOVEMENT AND ACTIVITY (such as the energy of a mind) as opposed to the imitative cinematography, the fuss and hysterics of the Futurists.' So he learned modernity from the Futurists, but loathed their blurred technique; he learned his formal structures from the Cubists, but felt them too limited ('HOWEVER MUSICAL OR VEGETARIAN A MAN MAY BE, HIS LIFE IS NOT SPENT EXCLUSIVELY AMONG APPLES AND MANDOLINES'); he learned power from the Expressionists, but started not from emotion but from 'the physical and the concrete' ('Give me the *outside* of all things. I am a fanatic for the external of things'). Vorticism is the one serious artistic philosophy to originate in Britain at this time, and it penetrated all the arts.

David Bomberg (1890–1957) exhibited with the Vorticists. His painting *Mud Bath* was first shown in 1914, though it is not quite

13

clear how long before this it was actually painted. It is a bold design, strongly geometric, built out of the interaction of crank-like forms. At the time he was potentially the most outstanding of the young avant-garde painters, but financial stringency and disillusion overcame him and he never quite fulfilled this promise.

Jacob Epstein (1880–1959), a figure who attracted controversy, was another of the group. *Rock Drill* (1913–14) has a direct relevance to the approach of war. He himself wrote (J. Epstein, *An Autobiography*, London 1955): 'My ardour for machinery (short-lived) expended itself upon the purchase of an actual drill, second-hand, and upon this I made and mounted a machine-like robot, visored, menacing, and carrying within itself its progeny, protectively ensconced. Here is the armed, sinister figure of today and tomorrow. No humanity, only the terrible Frankenstein's monster we have made ourselves into.' It is a grim realization of mechanized man.

2

The Outbreak of War

ON 28 June 1914 South Slav nationalists assassinated Archduke Ferdinand of Austria at Sarajevo. On 28 July Austria declared war on Serbia. Russia mobilized. Germany, which had been involved in a Triple Alliance with Austria and Italy since 1882, declared war on Russia and France, and advanced into neutral Belgium. On 4 August, Britain, because of her part in the Triple Entente with Russia and France, declared war on Germany. Grey, the British Foreign Secretary, in a still memorable phase, pronounced 'The lamps are going out all over Europe; we shall not seen them lit again in our lifetime.'

The war was expected by most people to be short, but Kitchener thought otherwise. He took office as Secretary of State for War on 6 August 1914. The regular army then consisted of 450,000 men of whom some 118,000 were serving in India and elsewhere overseas. In addition, there were Territorial Reserves of 250,000. Kitchener demanded an immediate increase of half a million troops; privately he was aiming at a million. Conscription was anathema to the non-conformist conscience which guided British public life; so voluntary enlistment—under pressure—was the order of the day. The first 100,000 were called for on 7 August. By September enrolments had actually reached 439,000 and in the last months of 1914 there were altogether 1,186,330 enlisted.

The Germans advanced swiftly through Belgium and by 6 September were within range of Paris. The Allies—Britain, France and Austria—counter-attacked on the Marne and drove the Germans back to the Aisne. By the middle of October there was stalemate; the armies dug themselves in, literally and metaphorically. Intensive German attacks at Ypres and Arras made no essential change beyond

15

adding to the death and destruction which was now evident on all sides. Trench-warfare had come, seemingly to stay indefinitely.

This was not the only front. Japan joined the Allies on 22 August; Germany was soon ousted from the Pacific, and suffered a disastrous naval defeat off the Falkland Isles on 8 December. Her U-boats began to range the seas and attack all Allied shipping. The sinking of the *Lusitania* in May the following year was treated as a crime; it now seems clear that she was carrying war-material, but the Allies got more mileage out of their propaganda than did the Germans. On 1 November 1914 Turkey entered the war, and engaged with Russia in the Caucasus. This led to Britain's military operations in Mesopotamia and to the sorry escapade of Gallipoli.

There was little clear vision of what it was all about. Goldsworthy Lowes Dickinson at Cambridge put the matter with depressing accuracy:

To me the worst kind of disillusionment was that connected with universities and historians. Hardly a voice was raised from those places and persons to maintain the light of truth. Like the rest, moved by passion, by fear, by the need to be in the swim, those who should have been the leaders followed the crowd down a steep place. . . . I learned once for all that students, those whose business it would seem to be to keep the light of truth burning in a storm, are like other men, blindly patriotic, savagely vigilant, cowardly and false when public opinion once begins to run strong. The younger dons and even the older ones disappeared into war work. All discussion, all pursuit of truth ceased as in a moment. To win the war or to hide safely among the winners became the only preoccupation. Abroad was heard only the sound of the guns, at home only the ceaseless patter of a propaganda utterly indifferent to the truth.

This was not a particularly radical view. Lowes Dickinson was an established figure who patently believed in perpetuating the class-structure and his indictment is the more powerful for this reason.

The establishment's literary response to the outbreak of war shows a similar and remarkable blindness.

'It must be remembered,' wrote Sir Herbert Read retrospectively, 'that in 1914 our conception of war was completely unreal. We had vague childish memories of the Boer War, and from these and from a general diffusion of Kiplingesque sentiments, we managed to infuse into war a decided element of adventurous romance. War still appealed to the imagination.'

Horatio Bottomley was the greatest of all climbers-on-of-bandwagons. He was quick to realise that patriotism was good business: he in fact netted some £27,000 from lecturing about the war. In August 1914 he had twenty racehorses stranded in Ostend; he got them back by offering the War Office any animals of use to them—not that racehorses were major weapons of war. On 14 September he opened a Patriotic Rally of the John Bull League at the London Opera House. He proposed four conditions of peace:

1. The handing over of the German Fleet.
2. Payment of indemnity to cover the cost of the war.
3. The partition of the German Empire into small States.
4. The dethronement of the Kaiser.

Bottomley was important as an index of public opinion, a master of the obvious. But not always. In one of his innumerable lawsuits, in November 1914, he claimed that a war lyric which he had just written in *John Bull* was better than *Paradise Lost*. This was not obvious to anyone but Bottomley.

Newbolt's attitude was characteristic of the generation. History did not change; he still wanted to 'keep the Nelson touch'. War was a game, like cricket, as in his unfortunately best-known verses 'Vitaï Lampada'. Even after the war, expressing his satisfaction at the commemorative inscriptions he had composed, and contemplating a new one for Gallipoli, he could write 'What fun we've had!'

John Oxenham, whose characteristically entitled *Bees in Amber: A Little Book of Thoughtful Verse* before the war had run quickly into fourteen editions, now produced the equally characteristic *All's Well! Some Helpful Verses for the Dark Days of War*, extolling the fact that to die 'Fighting for God, and Right and Liberty', not to mention 'a world's morality', is itself Immortality. He was still at it after the war with *All Clear! A Book of Verse Commemorative of the Great Peace* with hymns of praise for Christ's return, a smooth and easy reduction of four years of agony, and another best-seller. *Poems of the Great War*, sold for the Prince of Wales's National Relief Fund, had run into a second edition by September 1914. It brought together poems from the periodicals and it is hard to distinguish one voice from another. Here is Bridges, the Poet Laureate.

17

> Thou careless, awake!
>   Thou peacemaker, fight!
> Stand, England, for honour,
>   And God guard the Right!

Here is the drum-thumping Henry Newbolt:

> Then let memory tell thy heart;
>   ''England! what thou wert, thou art!''
> Gird thee with thine ancient might,
> Forth! and God defend the Right!

Here is Owen Seaman:

> England, in this great fight to which you go
>   Because, where Honour calls you, go you must,
> Be glad, whatever comes, at least to know
>   You have your quarrel just.

Seaman's phrase, in the same poem, about 'storied scutcheons' shows that he is utterly blind to present realities. With similar blindness Vernède calls for Armada weather and Fagan invokes Drake. Most of the poets make facile play with religion. William Watson, a writer whose craftsmanship merits rediscovery, in rebuking similar German professions, implicitly rebukes these too.

> We do not with God's name make wanton play;
>   We are not on such easy terms with Heaven . . .

Eliot was surely right in saying that in such writers 'the lack of curiosity in technical matters . . . is only an indication of their lack of curiosity in moral matters.' Jack Squire's contemporary comment is pertinent:

> God heard the embattled nations sing and shout
> 'Gott Strafe England!' and 'God save the King!'
> God this, God that, and God the other thing—
> 'Good God!' said God, 'I've got my work cut out.'
>
> (J.C. Squire, *The Survival of the Fittest*, London 1916)

Perhaps the most famous poem of this early phase of the war was Julian Grenfell's 'Into Battle'. Grenfell (1880–1915) was an aristocrat, son of Lord Desborough, and a recruit to the cavalry. His verse-form and sentiments are as anachronistic as was his regiment, but he says with feeling and sincerity what he stood for:

The naked earth is warm with Spring,
　　And with green grass and bursting trees
Leans to the sun's gaze glorying
　　And quivers in the sunny breeze;
And Life is Colour and Warmth and Light,
　　And a striving ever more for these;
And he is dead who will not fight;
　　And who dies fighting has increase . . .

The thundering line of battle stands,
　　And in the air Death moans and sings;
But Day shall clasp him with strong hands,
　　And Night shall fold him in soft wings.

(*The Times*, 27 May 1915)

'Grenfell', says Merryn Williams of this poem, 'uses images like sun, trees, grass, earth, colour, warmth and light to create the impression that a soldier's dangerous life is the only natural and good one.' Grenfell was himself full of ambiguities. In a curious way, as his letters show, he loved the war; at the same time he found in himself a love suddenly blazing up for those he was engaged in killing.

Rupert Brooke (1887–1915) was the representative poet of the beginning of the war. He had grown to be the darling of Cambridge and the leading member of Eddie Marsh's Georgian poets. Even Sassoon held his breath before 'a being singled out for some transplendent performance, some enshrined achievement'. He had an undoubted gift for flowing rhythms and memorable phrases, and these things are not small, but his waters flow swiftly rather than running deep. I. A. Richards said that his poetry had no inside. He turned away from a civilization on the verge of collapse to a romantic countryside or a sentimental love or a whimsical humour. He had, on his own admission, abandoned rationality for intuition. When war came he joined up with a schoolboyish fervour in the Naval Division and died on his way to Gallipoli. There is no better experience of the mood of the time than the five sonnets entitled '1914', idealistic, memorable and terribly, terribly naive:

Now, God be thanked Who has matched us with His hour,
　　And caught our youth, and wakened us from sleeping . . .;

As we read them now they leave a sense of pathos for the blindness of their smooth ease. Yet he was 27, and should have grown out of his

19

callowness. It is unfortunate that the last and best-known is the worst of the sequence:

> If I should die, think only this of me:
>> That there's some corner of a foreign field
> That is for ever England. . . .

Pinto made a trenchant comparison of this with Hardy's 'Drummer Hodge' from the Boer War:

> Yet portion of that unknown plain
>> Will Hodge for ever be;
> His homely Northern breast and brain
>> Grow to some Southern tree,
> And strange-eyed constellations reign
>> His stars eternally.

(T. Hardy, Collected Poems, London 1968)

It is simply not true that Brooke's grave on Skyros is forever England. But the English dead in South Africa do lie in earth from which spring trees strange to them under skies with constellations strange to them. The one sentiment, however sincere, is artificial and self-induced. The other is real. Brooke was living, and dying, in an unreal world which was swept away by the brutal realities of war. Yet we must not underestimate him. Bergonzi wrote well of the sonnets: 'They are works of very great mythic power, since they formed a unique focus for what the English felt, or wanted to feel in 1914–15; they crystallize the powerful archetype of Brooke, the young Apollo, in his sacrificial role of the hero-as-victim.' And their reception both shows the popular mood, and helped to create an audience for later (and unfortunately often inferior) verse. Churchill wrote his obituary in *The Times* on 26 April, 1915. 'A voice had become audible, a note had been struck, more true, more thrilling, more able to do justice to the nobility of our youth in arms engaged in this present war, than any other—more able to express their thoughts of self-surrender, and with a power to carry comfort to those who watch them from afar. The voice had been swiftly stilled. Only the echoes and the memory remain; but this will linger.' He was right: for all Brooke's weaknesses, linger it does.

Thomas Hardy (1840–1928) was one of perhaps two poets who actually realized what was happening. Already in his seventies he had

1. *The Merry Go Round*, Mark Gertler, 1916

2. *The Mud Bath*, David Bomberg

3. *W. B. Yeats, Sir Hugh Lane, J. M. Synge, Lady Gregory*, William Orpen

4. *Oppy Wood: Evening,* John Nash

5. *The Menin Road,* Paul Nash

6. *Ypres Salient at Night*, Paul Nash

7. *We are Making a New World*, Paul Nash

8. *Dover Harbour in War*, Wilson Steer, 1918

9. *Gassed*, John Singer Sargent

10. *A Battery Shelled*, Wyndham Lewis, 1919

11. *Unknown Soldier*, William Orpen
12. *Youth Mourning*, George Clausen, *c.* 1916

13. *La Mitrailleuse*, Richard Nevinson

14. *After a Push*, Richard Nevinson

15. *Travoys with Wounded Soldiers arriving at a Dressing Station at Smol,*
Macedonia, Stanley Spencer, 1919

16. *Swan Upping at Cookham*, Stanley Spencer

17. *The Rock Drill*, Jacob Epstein, 1913/14

18. *Ennui*, Walter Sickert, 1913

19. *Mrs Mounter at the Breakfast Table*, Harold Gilman, 1917

20. *Ivy Cottage, Coldharbour*, Lucien Pissarro, 1916

21. *The Vorticists at the Restaurant de la Tour Eiffel*, William Roberts

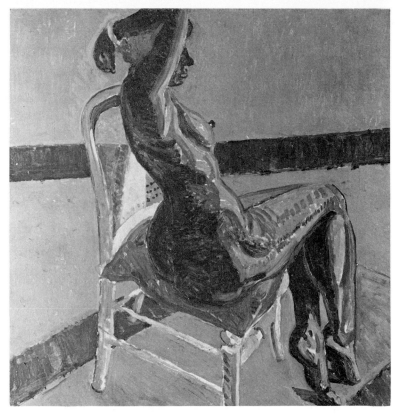

22. *Fitzroy St. Nude*, Matthew Smith

23. *Dinner Time, Men of the Royal Field Artillery near Frevent, June 1917*,
Muirhead Bone

developed an almost prophetic vision, and in 'The Convergence of the Twain' (1912) and 'Channel Firing' (early 1914) there seem to be premonitions of disaster. On 5 September 1914 he wrote 'Men who March Away':

> Hence the faith and fire within us
> Men who march away
> Ere the barn-cocks say
> Dawn is growing grey
> To hazards whence no tears can win us;
> Hence the faith and fire within us
> Men who march away.

op. cit.

The marching-rhythm contrasts with the irrelevance of Brooke's sonnet form. Hardy does not underestimate the faith and fire with which men went to war, but he sees it grimly, not gaily, and is right to do so. One of his most interesting poems is 'In Time of the Breaking of Nations'. In 1870, at the time of the Franco-Prussian War, he was in Cornwall and saw and was moved by the sight of an old man working in a field, but it was not till 1914 that he wrote the poem incorporating the experience. As war is recurrent, so is country-life permanent.

The other realist was Charles Hamilton Sorley (1895–1915). Eight years younger than Brooke, he showed a judgement far more mature, and had already revealed his gifts as a poet at school. He saw clearly how the smooth versification of the Georgians masked an emptiness of sentiment. 'The voice of our poets and men of letters is finely framed and sweet to hear; it teems with sharp saws and rich sentiment; it is a marvel of delicate technique; it pleases, it flatters, it charms, it soothes, it is a living lie.' Sorley wrote sonnets, like Brooke, but they are harsh not easy, agonized not heroic:

> When you see millions of the mouthless dead
> Across your dreams in pale battalions go,
> Say not soft things as other men have said,
> That you'll remember. For you need not so.
> Give them not praise. For, deaf, how should they know
> It is not curses heaped on each gashed head?
> Nor tears. The blind eyes see not your tears flow.
> Nor honour. It is easy to be dead . . .

> (C. H. Sorley, *Marlborough and Other Poems*, Cambridge)

It may not be great poetry, though it is good—as the light flow of the last line debunkingly follows a line of halting monosyllables, but it is unquestionably real. Sorley was capable of profound insight and an empathy with the enemy, which was totally at variance with the current popular view, encouraged by virulent anti-German propaganda, as we can see in his sonnet entitled 'To Germany'.

> You are blind like us. Your hurt no man designed,
> And no man claimed the conquest of your land.
> But, gropers both through fields of thought confined,
> We stumble and we do not understand.
> You only saw your future dimly planned,
> And we, the tapering paths of our own mind,
> And in each other's dearest ways we stand,
> And hiss and hate. And the blind fight the blind.
>
> When it is peace, then we may view again
> With new-won eyes each other's truer form,
> And wonder. Grown more loving-kind and warm
> We'll grasp firm hands and laugh at the old pain,
> When it is peace. But until peace, the storm,
> The darkness, and the thunder and the rain.
>
> (C. H. Sorley, *Marlborough and Other Poems*, Cambridge)

Sorley was destoyed by this annihilating storm.

Immediate reaction to the outbreak of war among musicians was a sense that all musical activity would stop until the war was over. Most of the festivals which meant so much to English provincial life were adjourned *sine die*. To professional musicians the prospects looked bleak. An article in *The Musical Times* on 1 September 1914 put the issues clearly. 'It is not only that the sudden and alarming restriction of means on the part of practically every section of the community forces even hitherto well-to-do people to question expenditure, but that the intense obsession of the mind in following the evolution of stupendous events produces a sort of stupor and a feeling that the ordinary concerns of life are jejune and insignificant.'

On 13 October a meeting was convened in the Queen's Hall under the respectable chairmanship of Sir Frederick Cowen (1852–1935). Patrons, composers and conductors, soloists and orchestral players and music teachers were there. A head of emotional steam burst out and filled the hall as present fears became mingled with past grouses. The dominant fear was of reduced employment, the grouse which emerged with it was against the preference of many managements for foreign artistes. Indeed, it was revealed that considerable numbers of English musicians were posing as Hungarians or Viennese to receive employment on fashionable occasions. There was a practical threat to security on the arrival of Belgian refugees. There was also a deal of jingoistic nationalism directed particularly against the Germans, but mixed with suspicion of any foreigner; the British have never been nice in disconnecting one foreigner from another. The result was the establishment of a Music in Wartime Committee charged with protecting the interests of British musicians.

One of those people who reacted most strongly against the suggestion that musical activities must come to a full stop was Thomas Beecham (1879–1961). Not only did he express himself on the subject with his customary forcefulness but, what is more, he acted on it. He returned to his native Lancashire and began to set the floundering Hallé Society back on its feet. Audiences dwindled in the first two winters of the war and Beecham continually dipped into his own pocket to meet the deficits. It was this constant generosity all through the war which led to his eventual bankruptcy. Even more important than his work with the Hallé, was his founding of the Beecham Opera Company early in 1915. Foreign singers had gone and Beecham was fully aware of the kind of task he had set himself. In December 1914 he said that it would hardly be possible to produce a first-rate Opera Company out of all the singers in England. 'In the first place, English singers cannot sing. There is only one I know who can walk on the stage with any grace. The others come on like a duck in a thunderstorm. I know of only one of whose singing a word can be heard.' Characteristically, he then immediately gathered forty singers, all but five of whom were true-blue Britishers, and by the end of 1915 had moulded them into an exciting, if unorthodox, company for singing opera in English. The repertoire was large and varied. Gounod's *Romeo and Juliet* was chosen for the first night; *Tristan* was an immediate success when it was added to the programme, while English operas included Ethel Smyth's *The Boatswain's Mate* and Stanford's *The Critic*.

There was an extraordinary ambivalence in the attitudes expressed in music circles; on the one hand there was a virulent opposition to all things German, and on the other a grudging recognition of the debt English music owed to Germany. Sir Hubert Parry's response to the war may be taken as typical. He had been a great supporter of Germany and German culture but with the war he came to believe that 'the hideous militarism of the Prussians . . . has poisoned the wells of the spirit throughout Germany.' He actually described the imperial eagle of Germany as a 'spatch-cocked carrion crow'. He called to Germany 'How art thou fallen from Heaven, O Lucifer, Son of the morning.' He saw the war as a righteous war, the British troops as heroic. On the whole he took the view that, although the Royal College of Music had to be kept going, *inter arma silent Musae*. But he favoured the exemption from military service of those with peculiar artistic sensibility. He held that music in wartime had four functions: first to console and inspire; second to express true heroism; third to protect the democratic spirit from the debasing effects of militarism; fourth as a distraction from horror. It is a conventional, establishment attitude, nonetheless sincere for that.

A lamentable example of prejudice was the way in which Sir Edward and Lady Speyer, patrons of the Queen's Hall Orchestra, were forced to leave the country for the United States. Musicians with German names or of German extraction found themselves boycotted and there were long debates about the morality of performing German music. The Queen's Hall policy in 1915 was amusing. They held two festivals, the last of the war, in April and May. The first celebrated the 'Three Bs'—Bach, Beethoven and Brahms, and to counterbalance it the second was a Festival of British Music, conducted by Beecham and (ironically) Emil Mlynarski. Composers represented included Frederic Austin, Bantock, Bax, Delius, Percy Grainger, Hamilton Harty, Josef Holbrooke, J. B. McEwen, Norman O'Neill, Percy Pitt, Cyril Scott, Ethel Smyth, Stanford, William Wallace and Vaughan Williams.

Even Henry Wood bowed to the prevailing wind. His Promenade Concerts had long had a Wagner night but in deference to public opinion he substituted a Russian night. As musical opinion changed later in the war, he brought Wagner back. Armed with the courage of his own opinion Beecham had a Wagner night in Manchester in October 1916 after the Somme slaughter. He actually gave a 'Parsifal' concert in Queen Alexandra's presence on Good Friday 1917, balancing the programme by rescoring the *Star-Spangled Banner* for the same occasion to celebrate America's entry into the war. In the same year Bax (admittedly somewhat detached from the war), inserted a quotation from *Tristan* into his *Tintagel*.

The ambivalence is spelled out in the letters of Havergal Brian (1876–1972). On 9 September 1915 he wrote to Bantock expressing his loathing for all things Prussian, and above all the Zeppelin raids. On 16 October he is acknowledging his debt to the Germans and admiring the courage of the raiders. The following month he wrote an unpublished letter to *The Daily Mail* deprecating the tyrannous hold of 'Hun Music'. But the following year on 8 October we find him writing to Bantock: 'Kling told me that there was an outcry against the German programmes of the L.S.O. It may be. But because we are at war, we needn't forget what the Germans have done . . . I certainly now—and always, shall look to them as my benefactors.' His comic opera *The Tigers* was a satire on militarism.

It was of course impossible to eliminate German influence from European music: it *was* European music. But even in 1917 (the year in which the Lawrences were extradited from Cornwall for her accent and his beard) Dr. Henry Coward, a respected musicologist, was advocating in *The Musical Standard* the elimination of all German music written since 1870. This idiocy continued into the post-war period and deprived audiences of a balanced view of musical development. Yet in a curious way it was not all loss: for the first time British audiences were systematically exposed to French and Russian music; more, it gave a chance for British composers to make their name.

The theatre, like the concert hall, felt the pinch at the outbreak of war; audiences fell away at first, but then gradually returned, in need of entertainment. F. R. Benson put on *Henry V* on Boxing Day 1914.

> Now all the youth of England are on fire,
> And silken dalliance in the wardrobe lies.

He had tried to join up, giving his age as thirty-four although he was fifty-six. 'Surely you are more than that?' said the recruiting officer. 'Are you here to get soldiers, or to ask silly questions?' rejoined Benson. Eventually he became a reservist in the Artists' Rifles which did indeed consist of artists of all sorts. But Benson's war-service lay in the theatre. In two months of the run of *Henry V*, over three hundred of his audience had joined up through the patriotic fervour he conveyed.

The response of theatre managers in London and elsewhere was to play safe and put on more revivals. The only major new production was Granville-Barker's version of *The Dynasts*, with Henry Ainley, a majestically appropriate piece. Meanwhile the provinces put on topical melodrama with villainous Prussians or sentimental domestic pieces.

The artists felt that the outbreak of war undermined their work. Sales dropped off. The very survival of works of art was imperilled.

In the first weeks of the war we find C. J. Holmes saying that 'the struggle between the enlightened or Christian nations' might be as destructive to works of beauty as were 'the wars waged by the barbaric conqueror of the past, whom we are accustomed to execrate'. He had the temerity to remind the British that they had destroyed the Summer Palace in Pekin not long ago. One of the more adventurous of art critics, R. E. Witt, went over to the Marne in the hope of rescuing works of art from destruction, and met much danger and hardship in the process.

Some of the younger artists were among the early volunteers. Among them Richard Nevinson was drawn to war, partly because his father had been a war correspondent, partly because Futurism had tended to glorify the gun, armoured car and battleship, and violence in general. 'The war did not take the modern artist by surprise,' he said in an interview in 1919. 'I think it can be said that modern artists have been at war since 1912 . . . They were in love with the glory of violence.' He claimed that when war came it found the modern artist equipped with a technique perfectly well able to express war. 'Some say that artists have lagged behind the war. I should say not! They were miles ahead of it.' So to the war he went in the Red Cross and the result was complete disillusion from the first impression of 'the strong smell of gangrene, urine and French cigarettes.' Still he thought that all artists should enlist, not because they owed England anything, but because a fearless desire for adventure, risk and daring would strengthen their art.

More traditionally *The Burlington Magazine* felt that art must be maintained, so as 'to keep alive these disinterested activities which are the distinguishing marks of civilization'. In fact the arrival of the Belgian refugees gave a fresh impulse to art, as some of them were artists, and exhibitions were held in aid of Belgium.

Not many artists were quick to see that war itself offered them new opportunities which had been little explored in modern times. Adrian Hill was one of the first; in the Royal Army Medical Corps he recorded what he saw, without genius but with skill and sensitivity. His painting *The Three Graces*, three dying soldiers, resting, not contorted, is a piece of poignant irony. And only one artist, W. L. Wyllie, discerned that the war in the air offered a fresh viewpoint.

Even in 1914 it was apparent that glamour and pageantry were things of the past, and that visually the story would be one of drab uniforms, mechanized transport, and a mudswept flattened countryside. C. R. Grundy, however, found a brighter cause. In *The Connoisseur* for October 1914 he wrote: 'The collecting of British military and naval prints is a hobby that deserves well of the country. Besides encouraging art it stimulates patriotism.' By the following year, when it was clear that the war was not going to be swiftly over, the editor of the same journal produced a thoughtful article on 'War and British Art' in which he suggested on careful historical evidence that the hope which some held that war would herald a renaissance in British art was almost certainly groundless. The Academy in 1914 had shown a combination of amiable landscapes, competent portraits, really rather nastily coy nudes, and pretentious sculpture. The mixture in 1915 was almost exactly the same, except for one or two canvases glorifying the British Navy. Even later in the war knights in armour are nearly as common as contemporary battles, and there are some deplorable allegories. Right in the middle of the war George Clausen (1852–1944) painted his really lamentable *Youth Mourning* with a cross on the left, a desolate scene of shell holes with blades of grass, and in the foreground a female nude bowed in grief.

One of those who felt, in an almost paradoxical way, that his art and the war were one was Gaudier-Brzeska (1891–1915). Gaudier had been an associate of Wyndham Lewis in the birth of Vorticism. He enlisted in the French Army, and from the trenches he sent back the following manifesto:

I HAVE BEEN FIGHTING FOR TWO MONTHS and I can now gauge the intensity of life.
HUMAN MASSES teem and move, are destroyed and crop up again.
HORSES are worn out in three weeks, die by the roadside.
DOGS wander, are destroyed, and others come along.
WITH ALL THE DESTRUCTION that works around us NOTHING IS

CHANGED, EVEN SUPERFICIALLY. *LIFE IS THE SAME STRENGTH,* THE MOVING AGENT THAT PERMITS THE SMALL INDIVIDUAL TO ASSERT HIMSELF.

THE BURSTING SHELLS, the volleys, wire entanglements, projectors, motors, the chaos of battle DO NOT ALTER IN THE LEAST the outlines of the hill we are besieging. A company of PARTRIDGES scuttle along before our very trench.

IT WOULD BE FOLLY TO SEEK ARTISTIC EMOTIONS AMID THESE LITTLE WORKS OF OURS.

THIS PALTRY MECHANISM, WHICH SERVES AS A PURGE TO OVER-NUMEROUS HUMANITY.

THIS WAR IS A GREAT REMEDY.

IN THE INDIVIDUAL IT KILLS ARROGANCE, SELF-ESTEEM. PRIDE.

IT TAKES AWAY FROM THE MASSES NUMBERS UPON NUMBERS OF UNIMPORTANT UNITS, WHOSE ECONOMIC ACTIVITIES BECOME NOXIOUS AS THE RECENT TRADE CRISES HAVE SHOWN US.

MY VIEWS ON SCULPTURE REMAIN ABSOLUTELY *THE SAME.*

IT IS THE *VORTEX* OF WILL, OF DECISION, THAT BEGINS.

But something had changed, and before the manifesto was printed Gaudier's arrogance, self-esteem and pride had been killed with his body. Gaudier's death set up a change in Wyndham Lewis's attitude to the war. 'This little fellow was so preternaturally *alive*, that I began my lesson then; a lesson of hatred for this soul-less machine, of big-wig money-government, and these masses of half-dead people, for whom personal extinction is such a tiny step, and of half-living into non-living, so what does it matter?'

One of those alienated from the war was the painter Duncan Grant (b.1885). When war broke out he was experimenting with Abstract Kinetic Collage Painting with sound, a long scroll of abstract, strongly rectangular forms to be steadily unrolled to the music of Bach. He showed it to D. H. Lawrence early in 1915; David Garnett records how Lawrence began to explain to Duncan what was wrong with his painting. However Lawrence was not unimpressed. The episode appears in the eighteenth chapter of *Lady Chatterley's Lover*, where Duncan Forbes is described as 'a dark-skinned taciturn Hamlet of a fellow with straight black hair and weird Celtic conceit of himself.' 'His art was all tubes and valves and spirals and strange colours, ultra-modern, yet with a certain power, even a certain purity of form and tone; only Mellors thought it cruel and repellent.' Grant might have been a major interpreter of the war, but his conscientious objection kept him remote from it, and he was directed to the country to work at agriculture. Artistically the war was for him a period of marking time.

Roger Fry concentrated on the Omega, a company which he had formed in 1913, with workshops in Fitzroy Square, to enable artists to make a living by craftsmanship so as to support them for the work of pure art; furniture and fabrics predominated, and some have argued that Fry's own best work lay in pottery. A quarrel with Wyndham Lewis, towards whom Fry behaved with a lightly calculated pacifism, did not help the success of the enterprise, and the outbreak of war hit it further.

Among the art periodicals it is notable that *The Burlington Magazine* continued to print excerpts from German periodicals through most of the war. Even more remarkable is that, as late as 1916, Joseph Pennell produced an exhibition entitled 'Germany at Work' at the Leicester Galleries, showing an unbounded admiration for the German industrial machine, and the German capacity for functional building. He got short shrift however from *The Connoisseur*: 'Mr. Pennell's regret at the action of "the brainless fools who brought on this woeful war" seemed chiefly inspired by the interruption it caused to his study and work at "The Pan Press in Berlin". If he chose to resume these labours, one feels that English art might possibly survive his absence.'

However, other prominent people in the visual arts showed they were ready—even in war—to learn from the Germans. W. R. Lethaby of the R.C.A. wrote a pamphlet on 'Modern German Architecture and What We May Learn from It'. He had been the adviser to a committee of seven men who made a report to the Board of Trade in January 1917 praising the high quality of German design and the organization of German industry. The seven were Ambrose Heal, Cecil Brewer, his cousin the architect, (a future director of the firm), Hamilton Temple Smith, a typographer, J. H. Mason, a metalworker, Harold Slater, a lithographer, Ernest Jackson, and a furniture designer, Harry Peach. They proposed closer contact between designers and industrialists with a view to raising standards of design. The result was the establishment of the Design and Industries Association, with notable benefit to British design. In turn some of their early material was actually published in German during the war by the Deutscher Werkbund.

Penrose's Annual is an index of the impact of the war upon lithography and other processes of reproduction for printing purposes. This work had been overdependent on chromo-lithographic productions from Central Europe, not least through the great Trade Industries Fair of Leipzig. These contacts were completely cut off, and with them certain raw materials, such as prussiate of potash, obtainable solely from Germany and essential to the bronze blue much used in the printing trade. The printing trade, however, came to take a nationalistic pride in developing the British industry, and it saw the war as a means of providing a protection more effective than any tariff barrier. The trade suffered, naturally, from the enlistment of trained personnel, though this again provided a stimulus to a higher degree of mechanization. The Board of Trade actually organized the first British Industries Fair in London in 1915.

The publicity posters used by the Government were a notable fusion of propaganda, technical process and some kind of artistic creation. Such posters had to command attention; they had to be attractive enough to hold attention; and they had to incite action.

The most famous of all war posters showed Lord Kitchener's pointing finger, 'Your country needs YOU'. It was well designed by Alfred Leete, it arrested attention, and convicted the conscience of many; it is sometimes forgotten today that England fought the first part of the war with a voluntary army.

One firm which was heavily involved in Government posters was David Allen of Harrow. The quantities involved were enormous and sometimes as many as 10,000 were reproduced in sizes ranging from stamps for affixing to letters or parcels, to wallposters of 60 x 40 inches. One of the best posters which David Allen did for the Parliamentary Recruiting Committee was TAKE UP THE SWORD OF JUSTICE. Justice is seen rising from the sea, a sea of drowning people as the *Lusitania* founders in the background. The colouring, and the design made up of a lurid sky, gentle funereal waves, and the swirling drapery of the goddess, are really splendid. Equally popular, but far inferior in design, is REMEMBER SCARBOROUGH: the town blazes in the background as Britannia leads a line of volunteers to enlist. Some of the best designs have the simplicity of the comic postcard. COME LAD SLIP ACROSS AND HELP shows a gigantic Tommy on the continent (a plain yellow) leaning across the Channel to grasp the hand of a man in civvies standing on a pink outline of Kent. STEP

INTO YOUR PLACE shows a number of civilians in the clothes of their trades and professions marching across the poster from right to left, to tag on to the rear of a seemingly innumerable line, increasingly khaki, which wheels and disappears in the top right-hand corner. A fine poster from the Central London Recruiting depot of 1915 shows a Zeppelin caught in searchlights above the silhouettes of St. Paul's Cathedral and Westminster. The message runs IT IS FAR BETTER TO FACE THE BULLETS THAN TO BE KILLED AT HOME BY A BOMB and JOIN THE ARMY AT ONCE AND HELP TO STOP AN AIR RAID. The pictures tend to simplify, to romanticize the soldier or the symbol, to caricature the enemy. Perhaps it was an essential aspect of effective propaganda. But not necessarily. One of the best posters was a straightforward lithographic reproduction ('beautiful and chaste') of the King's message to his people delivered in October 1915.

British war posters on the whole did not match their German counterparts. The one genius in the field was Frank Brangwyn (1867–1956) who designed some fifty posters for various charities without fee. It is said that the Parliamentary Recruiting Committee rejected an offer from him to do free posters for them: if true, it is a sign of remarkable shortsightedness. *The Connoisseur* picked out his 'Britain's Call to Arms', a lithograph, 60 x 40 inches, for special commendation for its masterly arrangement of black and white: a soldier central to the design is calling a man away from his wife and child to the devastation: he seems to be summoning him from light to darkness, but the light is created by the fires blazing from the destruction. This is indeed a fine poster.

The most notable opponent of the war was, of course, Bertrand Russell (1872–1970). He found it hard to understand the way in which Whitehead showed himself a fervid militarist, why Gilbert Murray wrote of the wickedness of the Germans and the virtues of Grey, and why J. L. Hammond, after years of opposition to war in Europe, was swept off his feet by Belgium. Russell joined the committee of the No-Conscription Fellowship, and later in the war was fined for 'statements likely to prejudice the recruiting and discipline of His Majesty's Forces' and deprived of his position at Trinity. Official reaction to Shaw's stance against the war was stronger still. Bernard Shaw (1856–1950), never one to swim with the crowd, wrote a manifesto *Common Sense About the War*. *The New Statesman* printed it on 14 November 1914 and ensured a circulation of 75,000. Shaw's first point was that the people of England and Germany were alike duped by their rulers: 'No doubt the heroic remedy for this tragic misunderstanding is that both armies should shoot their officers and go home to gather in their harvests in the villages and make a revolution in the towns.' But he did not expect this ecstasy of commonsense. Junker was at the time a term of abuse; he pointed out that a Junker is simply a country gentleman, like Sir Edward Grey. Militants were found in both countries. 'Therefore let us have no more nonsense about the Prussian Wolf and the British Lamb, the Prussian Machiavelli and the English Evangelist. We cannot shout for years that we are boys of the bulldog breed, and then suddenly pose as gazelles.' Britain besides had an extraordinary reputation for hypocrisy. Grey's tergiversations in fact allowed the war to develop. G.B.S. went on to criticize the conduct of the war, advocate Trade Unionism in the Army, and discuss 'the establishment of a Hegemony of Peace', a League of Peace. The churches had missed their chance: 'If all the churches of Europe closed their doors until the drums ceased rolling they would act as a most powerful reminder that though the glory of war is a famous and ancient glory, it is not the final glory of God.' Shaw favoured prosecuting the war, but not in a spirit of mad superiority. As he wrote later to Chesterton: 'What we have to do is to make ridiculous the cry of "Vengeance is mine, saith Podsnap."' Curiously enough the immediate reaction to the pamphlet was quite favourable, and the virulently hostile response which followed came more from a general impression than from a close examination of his actual argument. Robert Lynd wittily remarked that while nobody could take any reasonable exception to the pamphlet, there was a general sense that the war was a struggle of Great Britain, France, Russia, and Belgium versus Germany, Austria, Turkey and Bernard Shaw. His letterbox was crammed with filthy abuse; friends cut him dead; he was not allowed to contribute to *King Albert's Gift-Book*; he was warned off his clubs; the Press was forbidden to report his meetings. This naturally did not discourage the continuation of waspish, independent comments.

Two of the great publicists of the start of the century supported the war. Chesterton (1874–1936) as it happens was desperately ill. His physical resistance had been broken by the strain of the Marconi case in which his brother had challenged what looked like corruption in high places, and the bitterness of war. Not that he was a pacifist; before his collapse he had written *The Barbarism of Berlin*. In this he took a simplistic view, rejoicing in a knightly crusade against tyranny, and sticking to the simple facts of Germany's broken pledge in France and Belgium. He went on to write *The Crimes of England*, which he asserted lay in the past, in supporting Prussia against Austria, calling in Prussia against Napoleon and using Prussian troops in Ireland. This was not one of his better pamphlets (for that is what it was), the truth is that he was biased towards the little old German states, and towards the Catholic countries. This was certainly not true of H. G. Wells (1866–1946). In the spring of 1914 Wells had written *The World Set Free*, an extraordinary book which prophesied the atomic bomb with one hand and a world parliament with the other. The outbreak of war and his own turbulent life were strongly intermingled in his mind as he waited simultaneously for the birth of his son to Rebecca West and Germany's response to the British ultimatum. When he had seen the delivery of the first and the refusal of the second he wrote the article which introduced the now too-familiar phrase 'The War that will end War'. Wells was a mixture of contradictions. At one moment he was speaking of a war without revenge and a peace without passion; then he suddenly reacted into a state of jingoistic violence. Chesterton commented drily (for him) on the dangers of hurrahs too hastily delivered. Wells described Shaw and his anti-war pamphlet of 1914 as 'Like an idiot child screaming in a hospital', and himself looked forward to looting Berlin. It was among the stranger responses to war.

Hall Caine (1853–1931) was over sixty when war broke out, and had written the immensely popular *The Eternal City* in 1901 as well as the unjustly forgotten *The Manxman* (1894). He was wholly identified with the Allied cause, and his main war-work was fostering the British case in North America. But at the outset he proudly edited *King Albert's Book* and was made an officer of the Belgian Order of Leopold in consequence. He also wrote an account of the first year of fighting, entitled *The Drama of Three Hundred & Sixty Five Days: Scenes in the Great War*. The book is a curiosity, and a deplorable one. It has rhetoric without eloquence (two rhetorical questions in the first paragraph, and three exclamations in the third) and is infuriatingly egotistical ('I came to know (it is unnecessary to say how) what our Sovereign's feeling had been.' 'Not long before his (Ferdinand's) tragic end I spent a month under the same roof as him.') From here we pass through the Soul of France, The Soul of the Man who sank the *Lusitania*, The Russian Soul (and much play with the mystical word *Moujik*), A Province without a Soul, The Soul of Poland, through sections beginning 'What startling surprises!' 'And then Russia!' 'And then Poland.' 'And Italy!' (What have the Poles done to lose their exclamation mark?), to a final exhortation to pray for victory no matter what the New Testament seems to say. It is sad to see a good writer, a sensitive interpreter of the Isle of Man, pontificating in this vapid journalese, sad to think that his readership followed him uncritically into it.

Four major novels emerged from this period.

Ford Madox Hueffer, later known as Ford Madox Ford (1873–1939) was well-known for his brief editorship of *The English Review*, which fostered useful critical discussion of culture and society. He was to produce in the 1920s a mature fictional reflection on the war in the form of a tetralogy later grouped as *Parade's End*. He greeted the invasion of Belgium by the Germans with an Imagist poem, 'Antwerp', which T. S. Eliot called at the time 'the only good poem I have met with on the subject of the war'.

> Gloom!
>   An October like November,
>   August a hundred thousand hours,
>   And all September,
> A hundred dragging sunlit days,
> And half October like a thousand years . . .
> And doom!
> That then was Antwerp . . .
>
> (The Bodley Head Ford Madox Ford (8 vols.), London 1962–3)

In 1915 he published *The Good Soldier*, a nearly great novel, owing something to Flaubert and the French, a masterpiece of technique (its ease masks a balanced judgement and skilled co-ordination) yet in the end vaguely unsatisfying. It is, in fact, a pre-war book, begun on his fortieth birthday, on 17 December 1913. It is about the inability of the upper-middle-class English and Americans in the first years of the century to cope with ordinary basic human relations. The narrator has no idea what is going on around him; his wife is over-sexed and clever in deceit. The combination leads to disaster. Edward

Ashburnham, the good soldier, warm, altruistic but incapable of self-control, is equally incapable of controlling events. But so is the cool, skilful manipulator, operating within a more conventional framework, his wife Leonora. The innocent Nancy is a victim of their selfishness, incompetence and ineffectual altruism. The only way out is suicide, madness, or a kind of helpless acceptance. In a curious way the book took on new strength with the outbreak of war, for it pointed at the interaction of people's private and public spheres. These people who made a mess of their own lives made an equal mess of the world. It was emphasized by the symbolic date of 4 August on which the private disasters occur. Ford originally wanted to call the book *The Saddest Story*, and the opening chapters appeared in *Blast* under this title, but the new title also helped to establish the public dimension of the story.

Wyndham Lewis used the same period, during illness and convalescence, to write his first novel, *Tarr*, though it was not published until 1918. Lewis maintained that war and *Tarr* had dragged him out of his abstractist cul-de-sac. It is an unsatisfactory book, though Cyril Connolly numbered it among the hundred best novels. T. S. Eliot, reviewing it in *The Egoist* in 1918, said that it brought together the thought of the modern and the energy of the cave-man. Its satirical portrayal of emptiness of life opened the way for Aldous Huxley's brand of post-war cynicism. Like *The Good Soldier* it is about people who cannot control their sexuality and wreck their personal relations to such an extent that they destroy each other, just as nations destroy one another when their public relations have broken down and they can no longer control their aggressions. Set in Paris immediately before the war *Tarr* depicts the international Bohemian lifestyles there. While he is strong on portraying art-snobbery, Lewis fails to convey the fact that his characters are supposed to be artists. Had he managed, the book would have had a far more positive quality and allowed the irony to pierce like a poniard instead of smashing like a sledgehammer. The presence of Germans as an integral part of that community points the appearance of the book in wartime. Some critics (abetted later by Lewis himself) have seen in Otto Kreisler a precursor of Hitler or Goebbels. I do not see him so; he seems as pitiably ineffectual as the rest.

It is arguable that the best English novel actually about the the war and written during the war belongs to the early months. Hugh

35

Walpole (1884–1941) served with the Russian Red Cross on the Austrian Front, and succeeded in writing a kind of Russian novel in English, introspective, somewhat mystical, with an understanding of and insight into some of the complexities of the Russian national character. Its title was *The Dark Forest*; its central character the vivacious, volatile Marie Ivanovna; its theme was her relations with the men around her: the shy, ineffectual Englishman Trenchard and the confident, acquisitive Semyonov; and the background was the work of the Red Cross. There are splendid evocations of stretcher-bearing by night; of the empty, frenetic alternation of advance and retreat; of the boredom of waiting for something to happen; and of the oppressive environment of the forest in summer. The alternation of the narrator's record with Trenchard's diaries does not entirely succeed: it is confusing—perhaps deliberately, since Walpole seemed to want to superimpose the two Englishmen, and to emphasize the difference between the Russians, the gentle, strong, mystical Nikitin, the commonplace Andrey Vassilievitch, and the blunt peasant Nikolai. Nikitin's account of Trenchard is revealing:

'Why did he come? What did he expect to see? I know what he expected to see—romantic Russia, romantic war. He expected to find us, our hearts exploding with love, God's smile on our simple faces, God's simple faith in our souls . . . He has been told by his cleverest writers that Russia is the last stronghold of God. And war? He thought that he would be plunged into a scene of smoke and flame, shrapnel, horror upon horror, danger upon danger. He finds instead a country house, meals long and large, no sounds of cannon, not even an aeroplane.'

(H. Walpole, *The Dark Forest*, London 1920)

Nikitin goes on to discuss the Russian character, immediate, unrestrained, pessimistic, sentimental, tolerant to evil, passionately in love with good, not necessarily believing in God but curious about Him, intensely nationalist. Marie is killed by a stray bullet, Trenchard and Andrey by a shell. The unravelling of the threads is perhaps contrived—but it is also war.

D. H. Lawrence (1885–1930) reacted strongly against the war, (though he was liable to be suddenly captured by mass-emotion and to express a desire to kill a million Germans). His position was particularly poignant: he and Frieda von Richthofen were married on 13 July 1914. As the clouds gathered she had been to see her father for the last time: the old baron kept murmuring to himself 'I don't understand the world any more.' She and Lawrence had planned to return to Italy, but the war overtook them. Illness overtook Lawrence in the autumn of 1914—it was then that he grew his familiar beard which turned him in appearance from a young rebel to what we should today call a *guru*. He wrote to Cynthia Asquith that since the outbreak of war things had not existed for him. 'I have spoken to no one, I have touched no one, I have seen no one. All the while, I swear, my soul lay in the tomb—not dead, but with a flat stone over it, a corpse, become corpse-cold. And nobody existed because I did not exist myself. Yet I was not dead—only passed over—trespassed' so the official text: should it perhaps be 'trepanned'? '—and all the time I knew I should have to rise again.' He dreamed of an escapist Utopian island which he called by the Hebrew name Rananim. He wrote to W. E. Hopkin: 'I want to gather together about twenty souls and sail away from this world of war and squalor and form a little colony where there shall be no money but a sort of communism as far as necessities of life go, and some real decency. It is to be a colony built up on the real decency which is in each member of the community, a community which is established upon the assumption of goodness in the members, instead of the assumption of badness.'

Lawrence's major work to be published during the war, *The Rainbow* (earlier called *The Wedding Ring*) had been written earlier; he spent the first winter of the war rewriting it. The book has been very variously estimated. On its original publication it was suppressed as obscene: it hardly seems so today, though it is true that a passage of passionate lesbianism was later modified. Many critics are at pains to say that although they single out *The Rainbow* for special treatment, they do not thereby imply that it is Lawrence's best book; but clearly they see it as representative. It is in one sense independent of the war, in another it is a response to the war. It is, as Arnold Kettle puts it, about 'the living relationship of men and women, the struggle to achieve peace and fulfilment one with another within the colossal compass of the ranged arch of the visible universe'. Socially, it takes as its theme the impact of industrialization on British life. It is important, and a measure of Lawrence's prophetic insight, that he saw the analysis of industrialization as an adequate response to the war. Industrialization, imperialism and war were in fact a single

37

strand in his thought. There is a significant exchange between Ursula and Skrebensky.

'Do you like to be a soldier?' she asked.
'I am not exactly a soldier,' he replied.
'But you only do things for wars,' she said.
'Yes.'
'Would you like to go to war?'
'I? Well, it would be exciting. If there were a war I would want to go.'
A strange distracted feeling came over her, a sense of potent unrealities.
'Why would you want to go?'
'I should be doing something, it would be genuine. It's a sort of toy-life as it is.'
'But what would you be doing if you went to war?'
'I would be making railways or bridges, working like a nigger.'
'But you'd only make them to be pulled down again when the armies had done with them. It seems just as much a game.'
'If you call war a game.'
'What is it?'
'It's about the most serious business there is, fighting.'
A sense of hard separateness came over her.
'Why is fighting more serious than anything else?' She asked.
'You either kill or get killed—and I suppose it is serious enough, killing.'
'But when you're dead you don't matter any more,' she said.

He defends his position in terms of duty to the nation. She asks what he would do when the nation didn't need his services.

He was irritated.
'I would do what everybody else does.'
'What?'
'Nothing. I would be in readiness for when I was needed.'
The answer came in exasperation.
'It seems to me' she answered, 'as if you weren't anybody there, where you are. Are you anybody, really? You seem like nothing to me.'

(D. H. Lawrence, *The Rainbow*, Penguin 1968)

It is an acute satire on public school morality and its inability to come to grips with this world. Yet this same team-spirit sent thousands to die with extreme courage. Lawrence's answer to the search for meaning is a religious answer. In a letter of April 1914 about *The Rainbow* he wrote '. . . primarily I am a passionately religious man, and my novels must be written from the depths of my religious experience. That I must keep to, because I can only work like that.' The scene in Lincoln Cathedral, though Christianity was not his particular form of religion, makes the point, but Lawrence values Christianity only as it expresses something more primal in the cycle of creation. Fairly early in the novel Will and Anna are harvesting, in the moonlight, and there is a sense of physical rhythm which is at once part of the natural world and of their inner consciousness. Later Ursula has a mystical experience. 'It was a consummation, a being infinite. Self was a oneness with the infinite. To be oneself was a supreme gleaming triumph of infinity.' So at the last we come to the symbol of the rainbow, which in *Kangaroo* Lawrence called 'A pledge of unbroken faith, between the universe and the innermost.'

And the rainbow stood on the earth. She knew that the sordid people who crept hard-scaled and separate on the face of the world's corruption were living still, that the rainbow was arched in their blood and would quiver to life in their spirit, that they would cast off their horny covering of disintegration, that new, clean naked bodies would issue to a new germination, to a new growth, rising to the light and the wind and the clean rain of heaven. She saw in the rainbow the earth's new architecture, the old, brittle corruption of houses and factories swept away, the world built up in a living fabric of truth, fitting to the over-arching heaven.

(D. H. Lawrence, *The Rainbow*, Penguin 1968)

3

The Heart of the War

It was in 1915 the old world ended. In the winter 1915–16 the spirit of the old London collapsed; the city, in some way, perished, perished from being a heart of the world, and became a vortex of broken passions, lusts, hopes, fears, and horrors. The integrity of London collapsed and the genuine debasement began, the unspeakable baseness of the press and the public voice, the reign of that bloated ignominy, *John Bull*.

So wrote D. H. Lawrence retrospectively in *Kangaroo*. A. J. P. Taylor, writing as an interpretative historian and not as a creative novelist, showed how the mutual slaughter of the first year and a half destroyed 'the happy equation between civilization and victory,' and finally took the glory and romance out of war. It seemed rather that war would destroy the moral and material achievements of civilization.

Throughout 1915 and 1916 the deadlock remained, cruel in lives destroyed. From time to time each side mounted offensives. In March 1915 the Allies pressed at Neuve Chapelle; in April the Germans at Ypres; in May the Allies at Vimy Ridge, and in September at Loos. In February 1916 the Germans pushed again at Verdun; they 'bled France white' but failed to break through. In July the Allies counter-attacked on the Somme, with tanks: in some four months they advanced seven miles. Then towards the end of the year the French managed to regain some lost ground at Verdun.

The hardening of the war brought changes at home. In May 1915 Asquith had formed a coalition government. Lloyd George's energetic foresight at the Ministry of Munitions fulfilled needs far beyond the requests of the War Office. By the middle of 1916 he was in the War Office himself; by the end of the year he had replaced the fastidious Asquith as Prime Minister. It was an expression of the will of the people in a crisis against the Establishment. He was dynamic, devious, disreputable, but, as a war-leader, successful.

Meanwhile the voluntary principle had been steadily eroded, and there came a demand for military conscription. In 1915 Lord Derby was put in charge of a scheme by which men of military age attested their willingness to serve if called upon; two-and-a-half million men came forward. But even this number did not meet the demands of the war, and in January 1916 Asquith brought forward the first Military Service Act, imposing compulsory service on unmarried men between the ages of eighteen and forty-one with provision for conscientious objectors. The merits of conscription were—at least in the view of some critics—largely psychological. Aukland Geddes, director of national service in the last years of the war, said 'The imposition of military conscription added little if anything to the effective sum of our war efforts.' But it is important to understand the demand for it. It had become psychologically necessary.

By this time women were engaged in war work, and inevitably their fashions had to change. The extent of the change was well summed up by a postwar cartoon showing a little girl gazing at a picture of prewar fashion and saying 'Mummy, hasn't she got any legs?' Shortened skirts were the first sign of change—shortened that is from skirts which trailed in the dust and concealed leg, ankle and foot alike. Moralists thundered as efficiency, and shortage of material, lifted the dress six inches off the ground. Worse, girls working on farms actually took to trousers, and found them so comfortable that they continued to wear them after the day's work was done. The brassière, not unknown before the war, now pushed the camisole out of business. This was no doubt partly for comfort, but partly too for elegance, for the working woman had become more conscious of the need to put on elegance. So another revolution in women's fashion involved the greater use of cosmetics, and Arnold Bennett commented on the increase in the number of painted women around.

In the middle of the war slim volumes of verse continued to pour out from the fronts in Flanders, Egypt and Turkey. The poetry was heartfelt, but the writers lacked an imagination commensurate with the scale of the crisis as well as a technique capable of expressing it in words. One of the more proficient poets of this period was Robert Nichols (1893–1944), whose *Ardours and Endurances* (1917) became a best-seller. He was competent, but no more. We can trace in his verse the early romantic idealism, the exuberant response to the thrill of fighting, but no sense of tragedy, no despair. He did see, however, that the easy versification of the Georgians was unfitted to express the explosion of war, and attempted a style of fragmented impressionistic detail.

> Something meets us.
> Head down into the storm that greets us.
> A wail.
> Lights. Blurr.
> Gone.
> On, on. Lead. Lead. Hail.
> Spatter, Whirr! Whirr!

The American critic J. H. Johnston, has written a cruel indictment of him, with his 'febrile self-concern', and accused him of having 'no spiritual centre and no core of critical or evaluative intelligence'. That is overstated; Nichols is not wholly negligible, but he became self-satisfied, and ceased to develop.

While Nichols's stature has diminished, that of Arthur Graeme West (1891–1917) has grown. West reacted against easy sentimentalism:

> God! how I hate you, you young cheerful men,
> Whose pious poetry blossoms on your graves
> As soon as you are in them . . .
> > Hark how one chants—
> 'Oh happy to have lived these epic days' —
> 'These epic days'! and *he'd* been to France,
> And seen the trenches, glimpsed the huddled dead
> In the periscope, hung on the rusty wire . . .
> > > (A. G. West, *The Diary of a Dead Officer*, 1919)

That is an outburst of indignation, controlled and effective. In 'Night Patrol' the detachment is almost clinical:

> The sodden ground was splashed with shallow pools,
> And tufts of crackling corn-stalks, two years old,
> No man had reaped, and patches of spring grass,
> Half-seen, as rose and sank the flares, were strewn
> With the wreck of our attack: the bandoliers,

> Packs, rifles, bayonets, belts, and haversacks,
> Shell fragments, and the huge whole forms of shells
> Shot fruitlessly—and everywhere the dead.
>
> (*op. cit*)

It is this faculty for direct expression of realistic observation which makes us feel that West might have become a great poet. He died younger than Brooke; his vision was not clouded.

Until the war Edward Thomas (1878–1917) had been known principally as a prose writer with a poetic style. In November 1914 Robert Frost, whom he had met first about a year before, gave him the impulse to seek a tauter medium for his thoughts. Thomas's first poem 'Up in the Wind' was written in December 1914, and indeed the 141 poems which make up his poetic achievement were entirely a product of the war years. He joined the Artists' Rifles in July 1915 but was not sent to France until January 1917, and the intervening period was one of poetic activity. He was a patriot; asked what he was fighting for, he picked up a pinch of English soil. He loved the land and one almost feels that he was fighting for the land rather than for the people. Enlisting released something in him. Those who knew him said that his involvement in the war dispersed a melancholy which had shown in him before; but that melancholy is never far from his verse. The rhythms are subtle.

> The flowers left thick at nightfall in the wood
> This Eastertide call into mind the men,
> Now far from home, who, with their sweethearts, should
> Have gathered them and will do never again.
>
> (E. Thomas, *Collected Poems*, London 1965)

The poems are seldom explicitly concerned with the war; rather the fact of war has called Thomas to express urgently his values.

> The nettles cover up, as they have done
> These many springs, the rusty harrow, the plough
> Long worn out, and the roller made of stone:
> Only the elm butt tops the nettles now.
>
> This corner of the farmyard I like most:
> As well as any bloom upon a flower
> I like the dust on the nettles, never lost
> Except to prove the sweetness of a shower.
>
> (E. Thomas, *ibid.*)

43

Edward Blunden (1896–1974) was a craftsman-poet who also had a deep love of nature. Conservative in technique, but less facile than the Georgians, his work is relatively free from stock sentiments; he writes of experienced nature, not Theocritean artifice. F. R. Leavis said of his first major book that 'out of the traditional life of the English countryside, especially as relived in memories of childhood, Mr Blunden was creating a world—a world in which to find refuge from adult distresses; above all, one guessed, from memories of the war.' That makes Blunden sound more escapist than he was. He did not pretend that the war was not there but saw, rather, the permanence of the countryside as outlasting, almost absorbing, even the greatest of wars. It was a kind of creed, an assertion of religious faith. Blunden was a solid poet, who assimilated slowly and made his own what he assimilated. He was only eighteen when war broke out (he joined up in 1914), twenty-two when it ended. There is some truth in the thought that during the four years of war he was assimilating and expressing his experience of the countryside, just as in the years that followed the armistice the war was never far from him. Of course the war is there in the wartime poems, and 'Third Ypres' expresses something of the horror he felt; but the predominant impression of his writing at this period remains pastoral.

Robert Graves (b. 1895) has been called a 'quintessential Georgian' redeemed from the prettiness of the Georgians by his Irish background, which served to detach him from the English scene and to endow him with an inheritance of Celtic myth. Graves joined up early, fought at Loos, was wounded in the Somme campaign, but survived. His poetry *Over the Brazier* (1916) and *Fairies and Fusiliers* (1917) is free from the facile romanticism of most of the early writers, without ever exploding into the revolt of Sassoon. He is not afraid to portray the ugliness of war, as in 'Dead Boche'.

> Where, propped against a shattered trunk,
>   In a great mass of things unclean,
> Sat a dead Boche; he scowled and stunk
>   With clothes and face a sodden green,
> Big-bellied, spectacled, crop-haired,
> Dribbling black blood from nose and beard.

> (Robert Graves, *Collected Poems*, London 1975)

The metre, and the poetic devices (such as simple alliteration and colour imagery) are Georgian, but the rhythm and general effect are not. More often we have an effect of puzzlement, of disorientation, almost of a dream which becomes a harsh reality.

> The trouble is, things happen much too quick;
> Up jump the Bosches, rifles thump and click,
> You stagger, and the whole scene fades away.
> Even good Christians don't like passing straight
> From Tipperary or their Hymn of Hate
> To Alleluiah—chanting and the chime
> Of golden harps . . . and . . . I'm not well today . . .
>   It's a queer world.

> (R. Graves, *ibid.*)

Graves was writing about the war while Sassoon was still romanticizing it.

The other major poet of the mid-war, Isaac Rosenberg (1890–1918), was the child of Russian-Jewish immigrants, brought up in the East End of London. He was in Capetown when war broke out, loathing the talk of gold and diamonds, stock and shares. He greeted the war with some almost Imagist lines:

> Iron are our lives
> Molten right through our youth
> A burnt space through ripe fields
> A fair mouth's broken tooth.

> (I. Rosenberg, *Poems*, London 1972)

He was repelled by the war and yet at the same time romanticized it.

> O! ancient crimson curse!
> Corrode, consume.
> Give back this universe
> Its pristine bloom.

He did not reach England till 1915. He was alienated from the war, pulling away because 'more men means more war', because he held no strong patriotic convictions, because poets should not be sacrificed in that sort of holocaust, because to join up was 'the most criminal thing a man can do'. But join up he did, as a private. By 1916 he was in France and anxious about his writing: 'I am determined that this war, with all its powers for devastation, shall not master my poeting; that is, if I am lucky enough to come through all right. I will not

45

leave a corner of my consciousness covered up, but saturate myself with the strange and extraordinary new conditions of this life, and it will all refine itself into poetry later on.' That same summer he spelt out his poetic creed: 'Simple *poetry*,—that is where an interesting complexity of thought is kept in tone and right value to the dominating idea so that is is understandable and still ungraspable.'

Understandable and still ungraspable: this is the point. The more naive responses, like Brooke's, are too readily grasped, and therefore inadequate, whether as life or poetry. Jon Silkin has said: 'Rosenberg's strength as a "war poet" arises partly from his ability to particularize powerful physical horror and take it, without losing its presence, to a further stage of consciousness.' The astonishing fact about Rosenberg is that, whereas it took Owen or Sassoon some years of mounting horror before their response turned to true poetry, Rosenberg's finest war poem seems to have emerged, at least in its first draft, within about a month of his arrival at the front. This is 'Break of Day in the Trenches'.

> The darkness crumbles away—
> It is the same old druid Time as ever.
> Only a live thing leaps my hand—
> A queer sardonic rat—
> As I pull the parapet's poppy
> To stick behind my ear.
> Droll rat, they would shoot you if they knew
> Your cosmopolitan sympathies
> (And God knows what antipathies).
> Now you have touched this English hand
> You will do the same to a German—
> Soon, no doubt: if it be your pleasure
> To cross the sleeping green between.
> It seems you inwardly grin as you pass
> Strong eyes, fine limbs, haughty athletes
> Less chanced than you for life,
> Bonds to the whims of murder,
> Sprawled in the bowels of the earth,
> The torn fields of France.
> What do you see in our eye
> At the shrieking iron and flame
> Hurled through still heavens?
> What quaver—what heart aghast?

46

Poppies whose roots are in man's veins
Drop, and are ever dropping;
But mine in my ear is safe,
Just a little white with dust.

The masterful control of rhythm, the precisely observed images, the
sensitive imagination, the basic symbol of the roots show a sure
poetic hand. As the war rolled relentlessly on, a more hysterical note
infected his verse. 'Dead Man's Dump', written in the spring of 1917
is much admired, and understandably, but it is less finely controlled,
more brutal, leaving less to the imagination, and 'Daughters of
War', the poem he valued most highly himself, became mushed
down in symbolism. Nevertheless, Rosenberg had real gifts. Edward
Marsh, who patronized him but did not really understand him,
wrote: '. . . poor little Isaac Rosenberg, who never came into his
kingdom, surely one of the most futile sacrifices of the war, for,
except courage, he had no quality of the soldier and if he had lived,
he must have done great things.'

The outstanding literary record of the war is H. G. Wells's *Mr.
Britling Sees It Through*. He was working on it in the winter of
1915–16, and it remains one of his finer works. It reflects accurately
and honestly his own volatile reactions to the progress of the war, for
Matching's Easy is clearly his own village of Easton Glebe, just as
Britling (the little Briton?) is clearly Wells. So we see him pass from a
complex combination of disbelief, fear and expectancy through
despondency (Wells's own reaction after he had got over his shrill
anger) and utter pessimism to the emergence of hope and the
prospect of world government. The death of his son coincides with
the death on the other side of his son's German tutor. He tries to
write a letter from England bereaved to Germany bereaved, but his
mind is torn in the dialectic between war which divides and death
which unites. Astonishingly, Wells, the scientific sceptic, resolves
this through a kind of religious mysticism.

For the first time clearly he felt a Presence, of which he had thought very
many times in the last few weeks, a Presence so close to him that it was
behind his eyes and in his brain and hands.

Religion is the first thing and the last thing, and until a man has found
God, and been found by God, he begins at no beginning, he works to no
end.

Of course Wells's Invisible King is not the God of the churches. He is a cross between an inscrutable creator and a struggling, finite, imminent power. But Wells's mood answered the gropings of thousands—perhaps millions. *Mr. Britling* went through thirteen printings between October and December 1916, and the success in America was more fabulous still. It succeeded because Wells was at heart an ordinary man with an extraordinary gift for words. *Mr. Britling* lacks the prophetic vision of some of his scientific romances, and the war did not allow the humour of his greatest novels. On the whole it moves close to the surface, but the scenes are carefully sketched, the characters delightfully observed (Laurence Carmine is an amusing sketch of Cranmer Byng, the orientalist); and the words have power to stir the imagination and move the feelings.

Rudyard Kipling (1865–1936), who might have been expected to react constructively to the war, did little to enhance his reputation. He wrote a number of poems about the war at sea:

> Dusk off the Foreland—the last light going
>   And the traffic crowding through,
> And five damned trawlers with their syreens blowing
>   Heading the whole review!
>   'Sweep completed in the fairway.
>   'No more miners remain.
> ''Sent back *Unity, Claribel, Assyrian, Stormcock* and *Golden Gain*'.

His only major production was *A Diversity of Creatures* (1917). It is not Kipling at his best, except for one short story of the Stalky sequence, 'Regulus'. This dated from 1908, though one can see the reason for its appearance in the thick of war; it exalts public-school endurance and the refusal to compromise. Most of the sketches in the collection are pre-war; one dates from the outbreak; and the only two from the war-period are really ugly, especially the study in repressed hatred called 'Mary Postgate', which is told as if British airmen were never destructive, even of their toys as children, and British bombs never fell on children.

Ezra Pound, as an American, was able to dissociate himself from the war. In the early period he was still working out for himself the implications of his discovery of Ernest Fenellosa's investigations into Chinese poetry. It resulted in his discovery that the juxtaposition of isolated words could create a new significance. Fenellosa—or, rather, his Japanese instructors—had laid out the bare bones of a Chinese poem:

blue	blue	river	bank	grass
luxuriantly	luxuriantly	garden	in	willow
fill	fill	storied house	on	girl
⎧ white	(ditto)	just	window	door
⎨ brilliant				
⎩ luminous				
beauty of face	(ditto)	red	ponder	toilet
slender	slender	put forth	white	hand
in former times	was	courtesan	house	girl
now	is	dissipated	son's	wife
dissipated	son	go away	not	return
empty	bed	hand	only one, alone	keep

Pound turned this into:

> Blue, blue is the grass about the river
> And the willows have overfilled the close garden.
> And within, the mistress, in the midmost of her youth,
> White, white of face, hesitates, passing the door.
> Slender, she puts forth a slender hand;
> And she was a courtesan in the old days,
> And she has married a sot,
> Who now goes drunkenly out
> And leaves her too much alone.

Cathay: 'The Beautiful Toilet'

But after he published *Cathay* in 1915, Pound felt the need to produce a major work, and began *The Cantos*. At the same time he became interested in Latin love-poetry, and in July 1916 he wrote to Iris Barry about the need for more satisfactory renderings of Catullus and Propertius. This led to the brilliantly infuriating *Homage to Sextus Propertius*; brilliant because of his capacity to distil the essence of the Latin in a single phrase; infuriating because of his indifference to latinity, his impatience, and the grotesque unevenness of the resulting production. In a letter Pound said of this work that 'it presents certain emotions as vital to me in 1917, faced with the infinite and ineffable imbecility of the British Empire, as they were to Sextus Propertius some centuries earlier, when faced with the infinite and ineffable imbecility of the Roman Empire.' Yet for all the insistent irony, thick as layers of outdoor clothing on a winter's day, there was also a new poetic note:

> Shades of Callimachus, Coan ghosts of Philetas
> > It is in your grove I would walk
> I who come first from the clear font
> Bringing the Grecian orgies into Italy,
> > and the dance into Italy.
> Who hath taught you so subtle a measure,
> > in what hall have you heard it;
> What foot beat out your time-bar,
> > What water has mellowed your whistles?

We may cavil at 'orgies' but it is impossible not to recognize the brilliance.

1916 saw the publication of one of George Moore's finest novels, *The Brook Kerith*. Moore had said in *Modern Painting* that religious painting was certain of lucrative popularity, especially when bad. *The Brook Kerith* was a religious word-painting. Its popularity sprang from that fact, and partly from notoriety arising from the freedom with which he handled his theme. It was certainly not a bad book; indeed, it is written in a hauntingly mellifluous prose, though Shaw found it monotonous after thirty pages: 'It then began to dawn on me that there was no mortal reason why Moore should not keep going on like that for fifty thousand pages, or fifty million for that matter.'

Behind the stars that twinkled were stars that blazed; behind the stars that blazed were smaller stars, and behind them a sort of luminous dust. All this immensity is God's dwelling-place, he said. The stars are God's eyes; we live under his eyes and he has given us a beautiful garden to live in. Are we worthy of it? he asked, and Jew though he was he forgot God for a moment in the sweetness of the breathing of earth, for there is no more lovely plain in the spring of the year than the Plain of Gennesaret. . . .
But suddenly from among the myrtle bushes a song arose. It began with a little phrase of three notes, which the bird repeated, as if to impress the listener, and prepare him for the runs and trills and joyous little cadenzas that were to follow. A sudden shower of jewels it seemed like, and when the last drops had fallen the bird began another song, a continuation of the first, but more voluptuous and intense; and then, as if he felt that he had set the theme sufficiently, he started away into new trills and shakes and runs, piling cadenza upon cadenza till the theme seemed lost, but the bird held it in

memory while all its musical extravagances were flowing, and when the inevitable moment came he repeated the first three notes. Again Joseph heard the warbling water, and it seemed to him that he could hear the stars throbbing. It was one of those moments when the soul of man seems to break, to yearn for that original unity out of which some sad fate has cast it.

It is odd stuff for 1916, reminiscent of early Yeats, not at all of *Esther Waters*. Moore's reverent humanism is an answer to the religiosity called out by the war; his mystical unity is an answer to the fragmentation of the war; and his cenobitic Essenes, for the moment at least, inhabit his Utopia of reconstruction.

Lawrence too avoided the direct theme of war. He followed *The Rainbow* with *Women in Love*: the two were originally conceived as part of a single book. *Women in Love* was completed in 1916, but not published till 1920. It reflects little of the war, much of Lawrence's preoccupation with symbolism. There is some social satire, directed at capitalistic entrepreneurs, and some splendid descriptive writing. But, fundamentally, this is a novel about passion, and at the same time a curiously non-sexual exploration of the relationship between men.

At some date not printed in the book (not earlier than 1915 or later than 1917) *The Times* published its *Red Cross Story Book* by famous novelists serving in his Majesty's forces. They form an interesting group, none great, mostly good, some capable of best-sellers. Desmond Coke was to write some good school stories; Warwick Deeping became a popular novelist; R. Austin Freeman is best remembered for scientific detective-stories; Cosmo Hamilton was brother to Sir Philip Gibbs, and a miscellaneous man of letters; 'Ian Hay' had written *Pip* before the war, and was to produce during the war *The First Hundred Thousand* (which won a higher reputation than the writing deserved) and its sequels, and after the war to write successfully for the stage; Albert Kinross had been a journalist with a love for cricket; Compton Mackenzie was to become a dominant literary personality; A. E. W. Mason had written his best adventure story, *The Four Feathers*, and launched Inspector Hanaud on his career in *At the Villa Rose*, and was himself to have an equally adventurous time in the Secret Service; W. B. Maxwell was a craftsman in prose who wrote an attractive autobiography *Time Gathered*; A. A. Milne had been assistant editor of *Punch*, and had created the Rabbits, though Christopher Robin lay in the future; Oliver Onions,

Bradford-born purveyor of ghost-stories, was thirty years later to win the James Tait Black prize for *Poor Man's Tapestry*; Barry Pain was fifty when war broke out, a whimsical humorist with an established reputation; Quiller-Couch was even older, and had written *Dead Man's Rock* as long ago as 1887; Charles Roberts (later Sir Charles) was a voluminous Canadian writer; Theodore Goodridge Roberts was another Canadian; Ralph Stock was a wanderer who had made a name as a Tenderfoot; Martin Swayne had written three novels and was to write another, as well as an account of Mesopotamia; R. E. Vernède was a poet and a war casualty, killed in 1917. The stories do not enhance the reputations of their authors. They are slight and escapist, projections back into history, or into sentimental peacetime love or into aristocratic society, or the lives of idealized Red Indians, or the Canadian prairies. But this was what the public wanted.

The most popular writers of the period were Nat Gould and Victoria Cross. They had no literary pretensions, but they patently gave people what they wanted. Gould (1857–1919) ignored the war and was faithful to the same themes that he had written about before: the hunting field and the racecourse. Andrew Lang said of him: 'A Sixpenny Academy would be a lively Academy. For President, I would, if consulted, select Mr Nat Gould, who shines by a candid simplicity of style, and a direct and unaffected appeal to the emotions, and our love for that noble animal, the horse.' One suspects that he retained his pre-war readership, who enjoyed the illusion of normalcy; one suspects, too, that in the midst of man's inhumanity to man it was something of a relief to turn to horses.

Victoria Cross, pseudonym of Vivian Cory, later Vivian Cory Griffin, whose books dated from 1895 to 1935, was quite a different writer. She wrote sentimental romances about the upper crust of society, but was liable to prefix them with a passage from Euripides (in Greek) or quote from Plato. Her most interesting book of the period was *Evelyn Hastings*. It has an idealized heroine, and a war setting. Its fascination lies in that it is a kind of dramatized treatise on prayer, but it is not churchy—Evelyn says that going to church interferes with her prayers. It no doubt appealed to much wishful thinking from those who hoped that prayer would divert bullets from those they loved. Yet it has a kind of passionate power—and a delightfully satiric portrait of the mother, who lived by society conventions without real values.

Of the writers who had made their names with thrillers, Edgar Wallace (1875–1932) had an established reputation, chiefly through two series, *Sanders of the River* and *The Four Just Men*. During the war he continued his enormous output of novels in the same vein as before. The Sanders series, designed in their own way to extol British imperial government, continued with *Bones, The Keepers of the King's Peace* and *Lieutenant Bones*; the Just Men appeared in *The Just Men of Cordova*. The oddest of his wartime books, in being most at variance with his general writing, is *Those Folk of Bulboro* (1918), a satire on the sects in a country town; it is Wallace's concession to the revival of religion, and a double-edged one at that. He was, in fact, something of a patriot, and wrote a sketch of Sir John French early in the war and, afterwards, an account of heroic actions, and a popular history of the war.

E. Phillips Oppenheim (1886–1946) was described to his public as 'the greatest and most imaginative writer of sensational stories since Wilkie Collins'. This was nonsense: his characters are pasteboard; but he could spin a fast-moving yarn. But whereas Gould and Wallace stuck to their established formulas, Oppenheim, sensible of his own limitations, none the less saw that the war offered a chance for variations in his theme. He was too wise to turn his hand to the war itself. Instead he saw the situation leading up to the war as the opportunity for spy-thrillers without changing the established environment of his novels, and this formed the theme of *The Vanished Messenger* (1916) and *The Double Traitor* (1917).

A novelist who came to best-selling popularity during the war was Cyril McNeile (1888–1937), better known by his pseudonym of 'Sapper'. McNeile was a professional soldier, the son of a naval officer. After the Royal Military Academy, he joined the Royal Engineers in 1907, was given the rank of captain in 1914, and won the M.C. in the course of his war-service. Sapper made his greatest hit after the war with *Bull-Dog Drummond*, 'the adventures of a demobilised officer who found peace dull'. The success of the book and its sequels is as odd a commentary on one post-war generation as the success of the James Bond saga is on another. Sapper's best work was done during the war, in short stories and sketches of trench-life. These have few literary pretensions; they are simplistic in their outlook (but so was Sapper), and do not probe deep; but they are vivid, exciting, amusing and sometimes pathetic. Some of the stories in *Sergeant Michael Cassidy, R.E.* are delightfully entertaining ('The Revolt of the Cooks' for instance). In others he seems to be a first-class reporter. One little sketch, in which the morality as well as the draughtsmanship is outlined in plain black and white, draws an economical parallel between a bear and a German, both dangerous when their arms are raised in apparent surrender. Sapper is at his weakest when he introduces women into his stories: the contrasting attitudes of Drummond and Bond form a fascinating piece of social history; but his sketches of trench-life deserve to be rescued from the oblivion which sometimes falls on successful authors.

What Sapper did for trench warfare, Bartimeus (1886-1967) did for the navy. His real name was Ricci, but he took his pen-name from the fact that he was going blind. *Naval Occasions* was published shortly after the outbreak of war, and re-issued, in a new edition, in August 1918. They are sketches of life in the Navy—as the Midshipman remarks 'We *do* see life'. He followed this with *A Tall Ship* which consisted of sketches and episodes. Whimsical, pathetic, amusing and tragic, they recounted the response to the outbreak of war: the death of 'Torps' in action created almost as much sensation as the death of Sherlock Holmes had done in an earlier period and the death of one of the Archers in a later one. Bartimeus tried his hand at a full-length novel in *The Long Trick* (1917). It was a good move, for the short sketch tends to become a stylized caricature, and it enabled him to give an extended account of the 'feel' of a naval engagement in mist. Like many people, Bartimeus felt that the British Navy symbolized all that was best in life, and the mood he conveys is authentic.

The best of the popular novelists was unquestionably John Buchan (1875-1940). He had made something of a reputation as an unconventional historian with a prize essay on Raleigh, a history of Brasenose College written as an undergraduate, and a little study of the Marquis of Montrose. He had been assistant private secretary to Milner in South Africa, an experience which enlarged his vision and gave him an inside glimpse of statesmanship. The most notable of his pre-war adventure stories was *Prester John* (1910). The autumn of 1914 found him gravely ill and for the first time in his adult life he was compelled to be physically inactive. The mind took over where the body had left off: he wrote and wrote and wrote. He embarked on his twenty-four volume *History of the Great War*; and he wrote one of the finest of all yarns of adventure, *The Thirty-Nine Steps* (1915). It is a spy-story associated with the outbreak of war, consisting, for the most part, of a thrilling chase over Scottish moors, made convincing by Buchan's own open-air trekking, and vivid by his own frustration at being confined. Written in an economical style, it shows an eye for detailed observation. It took the reading world by storm; it was exactly what they wanted, enabling them to take a clearcut black-and-white, goodies-and-baddies view of the situation in which they were, to identify themselves with the athletic amateur against the clever but malign professionals, and to see the war not so much a massacre but as romance and adventure.

The success of *The Thirty-Nine Steps* (A. J. Balfour was among its admirers) made a sequel inevitable. This was *Greenmantle*. It is further fetched, the chief enemies being a woman master-criminal and a caricatured Prussian. But Hannay's reference to his experience at Loos and 'that awful stretch between Cassel and Ypres' made readers aware that he knew what he was writing about. 'The military details you touch on are correct, in distinction to many other war stories which have been written' wrote a soldier. The four heroes are excellent. The fantastic Sandy Arbuthnot was in fact closely modelled on Aubrey Herbert. The American Blenkiron with his dyspepsia and his patience cards is one of Buchan's best creations. The capture of Erzerum and the Cossack charge which end the book are authentic. It is a wry irony that the book was a consolation to the imprisoned Tsar. The trouble with *Greenmantle*, in context, is that it turned aside from the reality of most of the war to a vision of an adventurous, exciting escapade which was an affair of quite individual initiative, disguises, and cavalry charges, of fast movement and wide open spaces. For those in the Flanders trenches it was a liberation, but an empty one.

Buchan was one of several competent creative writers who also diverted their talents to record the war. John Buchan's *History of the Great War* actually occupied twenty-four volumes, and he added *A History of the South African forces in France*. Conan Doyle wrote his *History of the British Campaign in France and Flanders* in six volumes. John Masefield, who had attained some repute for *The Everlasting Mercy*, wrote unpretentious accounts of *Gallipoli* and *The*

Old Front Line. In this last Masefield tried to convey the sameness of the scene, 'dull to read' and 'dull to hold', as it was before the Battle of the Somme.

It is a difficult thing to describe without monotony, for it varies so little. It is like describing the course of the Thames from Oxford to Reading, or of the Severn from Deerhust to Lydney, or of the Hudson from New York to Tarrytown. Whatever country the rivers pass they remain water, bordered by shore. Soon, front-line trenches, wherever they lie, are only gashes in the earth fenced by wire, beside a greenish strip of ground, pitted with shell-holes, which is fenced with thicker, blacker, but more tumbled wire on the other side. Behind this further wire is the parapet of the enemy front-line trench, which swerves to take in a hillock or to flank a dip, or to crown a slope, but remains roughly parallel with ours, from seventy to five hundred yards from it, for miles and miles, up hill and down dale. All the advantages of position and observation were in the enemy's hands, not in ours. They took up their lines when they were strong and our side weak, and in no place in all the old Somme position is our line better sited than theirs, though in one or two places the sites are nearly equal. Almost in every part of this old front our men had to go up-hill to attack.

Such accounts could not hope to be objective, for the evidence came from one side only, and rather served the purpose of encouraging supporters of these writers to read about the war than of adding significantly to the reputation of their authors.

1915 and 1916 saw both a recession and a growth in music. The recession was natural, the pressure of the war was being increasingly felt. Less music was printed, fewer instruments were made, concert-halls were taken over for military purposes, fewer recruits were coming into the profession, private patrons were investing their money elsewhere. In 1916 Sheffield were still trying to sell the unused scores from the cancelled festival of 1914. In the same year English music suffered its greatest loss of the war when George Butterworth was killed at Pozières on 5th August. *A Shropshire Lad* had shown his lasting merit, and forms a kind of poignant anticipation of the annihilation of himself and others whose promise has not even reached that point of fruition. He was one of the few major composers in the front line; Bliss was wounded on the Somme and gassed at Cambrai: one other, Ivor Gurney (1890–1937) turned, as a soldier, from song-writing to poetry.

The musical revival was also natural. Those who had formerly gone to the Continent in the summer had had to spend holidays at home. Already in February 1915 the Harrogate Corporation voted £3,500— a lot of money in those days—for the orchestras in the Crescent Gardens and the Kursaal. Brighton, benefitting from holidays at home, was able to maintain its festival throughout the war, and as late as 1917 still had a permanent orchestra of thirty-two. In general, too, the war increased the desire for constructive recreation. Henry Wood maintained his Promenade Concerts throughout, and bodies such as the Royal Philharmonic Society and the London Symphony Orchestra had their reward in the response of enthusiastic audiences.

Little serious music of lasting quality appeared from British composers during the middle years of the war. There was Edward Elgar (1857–1934) of course, the uncrowned laureate of music, who felt some kind of obligation to write publicly for the occasion, and however genuine his patriotic sentiments, produced little more than rhetoric. *Polonia* (1915) and some of his settings of Laurence Binyon perhaps alone rise above the pedestrian. It was only in the last year of the war that he recovered his inspiration at the highest level.

One immensely popular feature of the period was the dramatic monologue with musical accompaniment. Elgar, in his *Carillon* (1914), had almost turned it into an art-form. For the most part it was heard in London music-halls and on provincial concert-platforms, in the form of tub-thumping patriotism, accompanied by martial rhythms and chords.

Elgar, however, retained a pugnacious advocacy of musical values. Bernard Shaw records an entertaining lunch party in the spring of 1917 with Madame Vandervelde, Elgar and Roger Fry. Elgar talked music so expansively that no-one else could slip in a word. Eventually Fry was able to comment 'After all, there is only one art; all the arts are the same'. Shaw heard a growl from across the table. It was Elgar, fangs bared and hackles bristling. 'Music' he spluttered, 'is written on the skies for you to note down. And you compare that to a DAMNED imitation!'

In fact Elgar's most obvious contribution to the musical literature of the war was produced twelve years before. This was of course 'Land of Hope and Glory' with words by A. C. Benson. On the night of 4 August 1914, once it was clear Britain was at war, it rang through the streets of London till dawn. In the days that followed, it was sung in clubs and pubs, music-halls and concert-halls and became a second

National Anthem. But Elgar was uneasy because he felt that the words 'wider still and wider' might be understood as imperialist expansionism. Another verse was needed, calling down divine vengeance on Germany, he suggested to Benson on 22 August. Benson's reply is of interest:

My dear Elgar, I'll turn to again and see if I can do anything but I'm not strong in the vengeance line, and indeed I don't see what there is to avenge as yet—we have hemmed Germany tight all round for years in the good-natured unsympathetic way in which we Anglo-Saxons treat the world, and the cork has blown out! What I do feel with my heart is that *bullying* must be stopped—but bullying mustn't be met by bullying and if we only end in being more militaristic than Germany, *je m'y pends*!
Anyhow, thanks to you, and I'll try again. Ever yours,
A. C. Benson.

Benson wrote a new version:

> Land of Hope and Glory, Mother of the free,
> How shall we uphold thee, who are born of thee?
> Gird thee well for battle, bid thy hosts increase;
> Stand for faith and honour, smite for truth and peace!

By this time Clara Butt was singing the original so persuasively that the new version never came into circulation.

Clara Butt (1873–1936) had a great sense of occasion, and combined it with sincerity. In August 1914 she had already squeezed the last drop of passion from 'Land of Hope and Glory' or even 'God Save the King'. One of her more remarkable occasions had been a concert on 13 May 1915 in the Albert Hall in aid of the British Red Cross Society. Hearing that D. A. Thomas, the future Lord Rhondda, was a survivor from the *Lusitania*, she sent him a cable, 'Congratulations on your lucky escape. Will you give me £1,000 for the Prince of Wales box at my Red Cross concert on May 13th, and fill it with wounded soldiers?' He did. The King and Queen were present; the National Anthem was played by the Brigade of Guards, in Costa's setting at the King's request with Clara Butt singing the second verse; Kennerley Rumford came straight from the front, still wearing khaki, to sing Edward German's 'Coronation March'; Parry was represented by his 'Hymn for Aviators'. After other popular songs came 'Land of Hope and Glory', with Clara Butt singing the solo unaccompanied, followed by silence, and then by the massive swell of the organ, the bands and 5,000 voices.

In March 1916, sensitive to the spiritual needs of the moment, Clara Butt organized a whole week of *The Dream of Gerontius* at the Queen's Hall in aid of the Red Cross, conducted by the composer, Elgar. The oratorio was preceded by his setting of Laurence Binyon's 'For the Fallen', sung by Agnes Nicholls.

> They shall grow not old as we who are left grow old.
> Age shall not weary them nor the years condemn.
> At the going down of the sun and in the morning,
> We will remember them.

Gerontius was a particularly exacting rôle for Gervase Elwes, but he stood up to it well. Clara Butt sang the Angel from a position, but not in a voice, of self-effacement. The hall was packed and many people had to stand.

Frederick Delius (1862-1934) one of the older generation of British composers, was hit hardest by the war. He was living outside Paris, his wife's home, when the German advance forced them to take refuge in Britain where he began his *Requiem*. Delius was not a Christian and wrote his own text, which incorporates Biblical allusions, but hardly to passages of faith and hope and, indeed, in places appears anti-Christian. This ran counter to the mood of the war and even of the years of disillusion which followed; its first performance had to wait till 1922 and was even then unsuccessful. Today Christians themselves are in the front line in the attack on churchianity, and it is easier to see the work for what it is, a notable musical response to the tragedy of war. There are two outstanding movements, the funeral march which opens the work with its exquisite use of wind instruments, and the elegy for soprano in the fourth part; the latter is a touch of genius, sunlight bursting through the cloud of war, and the sudden choral chant of 'long, dreamless sleep', as a backcloth is a lovely moment. Delius uses some original scoring in the *Requiem*, with triple woodwind in pairs and delicate writing for brass: at the same time bitterness prevents the delicacy from cloying. The baritone solo is not particularly memorable, and there are one or two awkward moments in the choral writing, especially in the third section, but it is a work of lasting value. War had the effect of eliminating some of Delius's vagueness, his misty soft-centredness; this is firmer, sharper-edged than his earlier work.

Delius's other work from the middle of the war is strong, almost classical in its form—as the *Violin Concerto*, the *Double Concerto*, the *String Quartet*, and *Cello Sonata*, all of 1916. It is almost a grasping of what is good in the past before it disappears.

Sir Hubert Parry (1848–1918) produced his two greatest masterpieces, among other important works, during the war. He was in his late sixties when it broke out; he died in 1918. In 1914 he had revised his setting of Shirley's 'The Glories of our Blood and State'. Death was already proving the leveller. In 1916 Robert Bridges, the Poet Laureate, suggested to Parry that he should write 'suitable simple music' to a song from William Blake's *Milton* beginning 'And did those feet . . .', as a contribution to national determination. He wrote the music and gave it to Walford Davies with the words 'Here's a tune for you, old chap; do what you like with it.' Davies later recalled the occasion—'he gave me the manuscript of this setting of Blake's *Jerusalem* one memorable morning in 1916. . . . We looked at it together in his room at the Royal College of Music, and I recall vividly his unwonted happiness over it. One momentary act of his should perhaps be told here. He ceased to speak, and put his finger on the note D in the second stanza where the words 'O clouds unfold' break his rhythm. I do not think any word passed about it, yet he made it perfectly clear that this was the one note and the one moment of the song which he treasured.' It became immediately popular. It was sung at the Albert Hall, and immediately accepted as the National Hymn of the Federation of Music Competition Festivals. It has often been canvassed as a national anthem since.

Parry's *Songs of Farewell* (1917) were 'the last and most wonderful of his choral writings' (as Hadow put it). In them Parry shows his gift for picking out texts from unusual sources. Campion's 'Never weather-beaten Sail' is familiar enough today, but there was a touch of genius in seeing its power in 1917. And 'There is an old Belief' was actually adapted from a letter from Lockhart to Carlyle. These two pieces have a rare spiritual beauty expressed through an unobtrusively masterful technique. It was appropriate that 'There is an old Belief' was sung at Parry's funeral; the whole work should be more frequently heard.

Ralph Vaughan Williams (1872–1958) was over forty when war broke out. He enlisted in the RAMC, but did not go to France till

1916. A *Pastoral Symphony* began to germinate in the intervening period in his mind; the great trumpet cadenza of the second movement was in fact suggested by hearing a bugler at practice. There are further reminders of the war in the last movement, where the sudden inclusion of the off-stage vocal line is like a lament for the dead, and the dialogue between woodwind and strings recalls the dead Butterworth's *A Shropshire Lad*.

On the whole, however, musically the war was, for him, a static period. War service absorbed him; he moved from France to Salonika and on being selected for a commission characteristically commented 'My only regret at leaving is that I shall cease to be a man and become an officer.' His musical reputation, however, did not diminish.

It is ironical that Gustav Holst (1874–1934) was working on 'Mars, the Bringer of War' in August 1914. The war hit Holst hard; he tried to enlist but was turned down on medical grounds and began to feel himself useless. He continued to compose, and 1917 saw the completion of perhaps his two most outstanding works.

The first was *The Planets*, a work whose varied sensitivity was enhanced by the various moods of wartime Britain, from the bestial savagery of Mars through the gentle romanticism of Venus to the mystic remoteness of Neptune. Holst's own favourite movement was Saturn, written in a mood of bleak desolation, with a technique ready to match the theme. He did not think highly of the work as a whole, which is indeed extremely uneven, but has remained popular for its positive qualities. The other was *The Hymn of Jesus*, unorthodox in its theological approach; Holst taught himself Greek in order to read the original, and visited a monastery to be sure that his

61

plainsong was right. It is a work of mystical exaltation; the dazzling radiance of 'To you who gaze a lamp am I' is its musical and spiritual climax. The work is highly original, yet in the line of musical tradition—for example he uses a kind of ground-bass in the earlier and later sections. The choral counterpoint shows how Holst had absorbed William Byrd, one of his favourite composers. There are some glorious touches of orchestration, such as the use of celesta, and an interestingly flexible rhythm. Some of the harmonies seem to sparkle; others are remote and mysterious. There is nothing finer than the way a strong 5/4 dance rhythm gives way before an ethereal Amen.

Only at the end of the war came the opportunity for involvement for which Holst was longing: the YMCA invited him to organize musical activities among the troops in the Near East. (Adrian Boult conducted a private performance of *The Planets* as a farewell gift. It was the first time Holst had heard the work.)

When conscription was introduced in 1916 the effect was to decimate the orchestras. The result, however, was not wholly deleterious. The symphony orchestras had been bastions of what we would today call male chauvinism. Henry Wood's Queen's Hall Orchestra was a notable exception; he had introduced six women in October 1913, insisting on equal pay for equal work from the first. Now the walls were breached and women were admitted. In three theatres—the Aldwych, the Coliseum (which retained a male tympanist), and Drury Lane, for example—in cinemas, in cafés, the orchestras were now often all female. Women made up concert-parties to entertain the troops. They had always had a significant part in revues and music halls, but it was during the war that Gwendoline Vrogden, Alice Delysia, Florrie Forde, and Vesta Tilley enjoyed some of their supreme triumphs. Alice Delysia popularized the best-known of the recruiting songs 'We don't want to lose you, but we think you ought to go' with music (as is sometimes forgotten) by the very reputable Paul Rubens.

Naturally light music was in especial demand. The London theatres were packed with soldiers and sailors on leave, as well as with those facing difficulties and shortages at home, all wanting their minds taking off the war. Paul Rubens's *Tina* (1915) was, as W. H. Berry put it, 'the stuff to give the troops', light, inconsequential, diverting, melodious. American shows with their strongly syncopated rhythms, such as Nat D. Ayers' *Houp-La!* and Max Darewski's *Hanky Panky* (1917), retained their popularity. And of course there were the evergreen Bing Boys. It was in one of these shows that George Robey and Violet Loraine made a smash-hit with 'If you were the only girl in the world'. G. H. Clutsam and Basil Hood asserted British nationalism in a Sullivanesque vein in *Young England* (1916); the more ponderous musical journals welcomed the show as a portent, but though it enjoyed some success it conspicuously lacked the genius of either Gilbert or Sullivan. The great successes of the war were *Chu Chin Chow* (*The Mousetrap* of its day with 2238 performances), and *The Maid of the Mountains* (1352 performances). the audience wanted escape, sentiment, some spectacle, lusciousness, tunefulness, and an absence of thought.

The cinema was one of the country's more important musical institutions. Films, of course, were silent; usually musical accompaniment was provided by a small orchestral group, often of a dozen players, but at least with a string trio, piano, harmonium and percussion. At the London Stoll in 1917 George Saker's orchestra was actually playing for six hours a day. Cinema organs were beginning to be introduced before the war (the first was found in Accrington in 1913) smaller cinemas had to make do with a pianist.

It is hard to say whether the overall effect was to raise or lower musical sensitivity. Certainly it altered it. Overtures and intervals could familiarize audiences with great music, though without the resources of a great orchestra; for instance, *Fingal's Cave* became widely known through the cinema. During the performance snatches of melodies from the masters would appear, and even if the audiences were deprived of subtle harmony and fine instrumental timbre, they received something. There was some encouragement to composers to provide suitable music for oriental scenes or galloping horses: programme music, but not necessarily to be sniffed at. More ambiguous in its effect was the tendency to associate particular scenes with a musical stereotype. Waterfalls were invariably matched with descending scales, with the result that descending scales out of the cinematic context became associated with a visual image of waterfalls, a fact that shows that cinema audiences took in more than they were sometimes alleged to do. Perhaps most regrettable was the tendency to treat all music as background music. However, through the cinema thousands upon thousands of people who would never dream of entering a concert hall had some sort of musical experience.

Out at the Front an interesting feature was the popularity of ragtime piano duets. The critic, W. J. Turner wrote: 'This should be comforting to those who maintain, like myself, that the natural uncultivated taste in music is better than the large commercial product which the public is induced to consume—for there is no doubt whatever that most ragtimes, with their syncopation, vivid rhythms, and frequently attractive modulations, are the best music that many people hear, and far superior to what singers of ragtime would probably refer to as 'high class' songs, meaning the sort of unmusical twaddle you may see advertised any Saturday in the *Daily Telegraph*'.

Jazz had become established across the Atlantic in the war, but had not reached Britain. In the autumn of 1919 the Original Dixieland Jazz Band opened a three months' season at the Hammersmith Palais de Danse, and *Tiger Rag* hit Britain. R. W. S. Mendl in his book on *The Appeal of Jazz* saw this as part of the war scene: 'Jazz is the product of a restless age; an age in which the fever of war is only now beginning to abate its fury; when men and women, after their efforts in the great struggle, are still too much disturbed to be content with a tranquil existence.'

Not surprisingly, the most popular music with the Tommies—the privates in the army—was catchy marching songs, sometimes sentimental, sometimes cynical. The most famous of them 'It's a long way to Tipperary', had been written in 1911, but had never really caught on. It was brought back into the music halls in 1914, and some soldiers picked it up. *The Daily Mail* reported this, the publishers used this report to increase sales, and efficient commercialism thrust it back at the troops. 'Keep the Home Fires Burning' was introduced by Ivor Novello (1893–1951) in one of Lena Ashwell's concert parties at Rouen in 1915. It would be hard to overestimate the importance of such concert parties to morale. Harry Lauder, the Scots comedian, was knighted for his contribution to them. In 1916 a young musical-comedy actor, Leslie Henson, of the india-rubber face, appeared in a revue in the new garrison theatre at Oswestry, together with Stanley Holloway, Davy Burnaby and some of the Gaiety Girls. It was a remarkable performance. They were at the Gaiety Theatre on Saturday evening, took the night mail to Chester, writing the revue on the train, rehearsed it on Sunday morning, and performed it twice later in the day. It was the sort of spontaneous combustion Henson loved. Later in the war he ran a company at Lille called 'The Gaieties'.

Many of the songs popular with soldiers were parodies, sometimes gloriously incongruous, of well-known ditties. 'Our little wet trench in the West' took off the popular ballad 'Our little grey home in the West'. 'You wore a tulip, a bright yellow tulip' became 'I wore a tunic, a dirty khaki tunic'. Pompous piety was a natural target. 'What a friend we have in Jesus' became 'When this bloody war is over', 'Lead, kindly light' provided the tune for 'We've had no beer, we've had no beer today.' and the cheerful profanities of 'Fred Karno's Army' were set to 'The Church's One Foundation.'

> We are Fred Karno's army,
> The ragtime infantry.
> We cannot fight, we cannot shoot,
> What ---- use are we!
> And when we get to Berlin
> The Kaiser he will say,
> 'Hoch, hoch! Mein Gott! What a bloody fine lot
> Are the ragtime infantry!'

One wonders just what the Germans thought during the Christmas truce of 1914 when their singing of *Stille Nacht* brought back this in echo!

Some of the ballads had a long history. The eighteenth-century 'Jack Hall', a narrative of a chimney-sweep hanged for murder, retained the essence of the story, but the murderer became Captain Hall; in the climax he finds the soapy Chaplain in Hell with him. Another, even more curious, history has been traced back to Johann Ludwig Uhland's touching poem about three German soldiers who cross the Rhine and find an inn with a beautiful dead girl who wins their love. The ballad unhappily cried out for parody, and received it, and in the war 'the Rhine' became 'the Line', and the girl restored to lasting life. There were British songs with nonsense refrains such as 'skibboo, skibboo, skiboodley-boo' or 'skiboo, skiboo, ski-bumpity-bump-skiboo' and these became attached to the sexual adventures of the German officer, as the three soldiers had now become. Out of this came the irrepressible 'Mademoiselle from Armenteers' with its 'inky-pinky, parlez vous' refrain. In all these we can see the development of a popular art form. Their cheerful bawdiness was an obvious relief to the feelings, their irreverence pulled officers, chaplains and stay-at-homes down into the mud with the troops, they had swinging tunes and catchy refrains, and above all they offered opportunities for creative improvisation. Some were not without picturesque beauty:

> Here's to the Tree of Life
> That ladies love to scan.
> It stands between two stones
> Upon the Isle of Man.
> Here's to the little bush
> That did that tree entwine.
> It blossoms once a month
> And bears fruit once in nine.

The soldiers were, in their way, poets who turned Sailly-la-Bourse into Sally Booze, Godewaersvelde into Gertie Wears Velvet, Chamblain Châtelain into Charlie Chaplin, and Auchonvillers into Ocean Villas, and who christened Hell Fire Corner and saw in a low hillock Stirling Castle and a sea of shell-holes Dumbarton Lakes.

Many of the songs sound, and were, cynical.

> Far, far from Ypres I want to be,
> Where German snipers can't get at me,
> Damp is my dug-out,
> Cold are my feet,
> Waiting for whizz-bangs
> To send me to sleep.

The most powerfully cynical of the soldiers' songs was 'The Old Barbed Wire'.

> If you want to find the CO,
> I know where he is, I know where he is.
> If you want to find the CO,
> I know where he is,
> He's down in the deep dug-outs.
> I've seen him, I've seen him,
> Down in the deep dug-outs,
> I've seen him,
> Down in the deep dug-outs.

> If you want to find the old battalion,
> I know where they are, I know where they are.
> If you want to find the old battalion,
> I know where they are,
> They're hanging on the old barbed wire.
> I've seen 'em, I've seen 'em,
> Hanging on the old barbed wire,
> I've seen 'em,
> Hanging on the old barbed wire.

So too 'The sergeant-major's having a time' took over some versions of 'Mademoiselle from Armenteers'. This cynicism was very different from the cynicism of Sassoon. John Brophy, himself a soldier during the war, put it well: 'These songs satirized more than war: they poked fun at the soldier's own desire for peace and rest, and so prevented it from overwhelming his will to go on doing his duty. They were not symptoms of defeatism, but strong bulwarks against it.'

The cheap portable gramophone did much to alleviate life in the trenches, and the military authorities of both sides regarded it as a vital necessity. Records of 'Keep the Home Fires Burning', 'Pack up your Troubles', 'Mademoiselle from Armenteers', 'Tipperary' had sales of about half a million.

In January 1916 Captain F. J. Roberts, who was responsible for the excruciating couplet

> Would you as a decent cove ack-
> nowledge yourself a Czechoslovak?

discovered an old printing works just off the square at Ypres. One of his sergeants put it in order. So was born *The Wipers Times* on 12 February. A shell destroyed the press, but the type was saved, a new press found at Hell Fire Corner, and, as the battalion moved round, the paper became successively *The New Church Times* (from Neuve Eglise), *The Kemmel Times*, and then (to avoid revealing troop movements) *The B.E.F. Times*, and finally in November 1918 *The Better Times*. Contributions are usually anonymous or pseudonymous. Gilbert Frankau was one of the few authors to sign his name. Some of the better contributions parody the columnists who had too easy answers (like Hilaire Belloc), or wrote so intimately about dangers they had not faced (like Beach Thomas). The verse, of which there is much, is light, ephemeral and jingling. One of the better examples is 'A "B.-E.-F." Alphabet'.

> A is the ARMY, in which he's a veteran
> Who's fought for a year from the Somme up to Meteren,
> Finding in Winter each week is a wetter'un
> And passing his day in the trenches.

By the time we have passed through Blighty, Cavalry, Duckboards ... Gas ... Kultur ... Minnie ... Pediculi ... Sappers, Trenches ... Whiskey and Whizzbangs ... to Zero, something of the reality of trenchlife comes alive again, and to laugh at it wryly was what people needed then. So the mock advertisements, the topical allusions in a personal column, the little snippets of Army slang (napoo, i.e. 'il n'y en a plus' 'there's nothing left', appears time and again) kept up morale. The attitude to the Germans is naturally simplistic: they are always Huns, and treated as comic rather than dangerous. The sheets had a wide circulation, but they express the humour of the officers rather than of the Tommies, since they continually recall the public-school magazine. They are a reminder that the ephemeral often has a more immediate impact than work of far finer grain, and has its needed place.

The cinema itself boomed. It, too, offered escapism, and attracted non theatre-goers. It was innovating and exciting. Wartime pressures drastically reduced the possibility of originating films in Britain. The result was a wide showing of films from America, which in its turn had repercussions on the British way of life. D. W. Griffith and Charles Chaplin were beginning to show the creative possibilities of the cinema, and the Mack Sennett comedies retain their slapstick verve, but for the most part the imported films retreated into a world of eminently forgettable artificiality.

Barrie and Shaw apart, the war-time theatre had little new to offer of any lasting importance. There were many revivals; managers, as J. C. Trewin put it, 'preferred to whip and re-whip the froth'. Lilian Baylis and Ben Greet kept Shakespeare going on a shoestring at the Vic. Sybil Thorndike, in the making but not yet made, had all the parts she yearned for except Hamlet. Male actors were at a premium, and she played Prince Hal, Launcelot Gobbo, Ferdinand, and the fool in *Lear*, this last white-faced with no eyebrows, a blank reflection of Lear's moods; it would have been good to see. The climax of the Shakespearian revivals was at Drury Lane in May 1916 when the tercentenary was celebrated by *Julius Caesar* and a pageant, and Benson was knighted in the theatre. (When asked whether it was Shakespeare's tercentenary or Benson's, the popular answer was 'It's the same thing.') There were other revivals too—Sheridan's *The School for Scandal* and Goldsmith's *She Stoops to Conquer*, Arnold Bennett's *Milestones* and Byron's *Manfred*. Ibsen played to full houses, and interest in venereal diseases led to the resuscitation of the topical but inartistic French play *Damaged Goods* by Brieux.

J. M. Barrie (1860–1937) is today an underrated dramatist. Sentimentality mars some of his work, but there is a rich vein of humour and an experienced sense of the theatre running through it. He had made his reputation before 1914, and in the war situation his work began to seem passé, an impression increased by the sickly sentimentalism of *A Kiss for Cinderella* in 1916. But then in 1917 came one of his major successes, *Dear Brutus*. Perhaps this was overvalued in its day, but it is the work of a master technician of the theatre and a creative artist skilled in playing on the mood of his audience. Of all Barrie's plays it is the most revealing of the inner workings of his mind. It is not too much to say that the war had driven him inward—away from the great external anxiety he felt about the fate of his protégés. Lob's enchanted wood is the perfect model of the unconscious, with Lob himself, the child remaining in Barrie, now controlling events. Mr. Coade is a kind of grown-up Peter Pan, and Dearth, Barrie without a wife. After this the curious extravaganza *Rosy Rapture* (1918) was a sad decline, and *Echoes of the War* (1918) four short pieces, left no impact.

Bernard Shaw (1856–1950) was slow to publish his plays, and his main publication of the middle war years comprised works written before it started, *Androcles and the Lion*, *Overruled* and *Pygmalion*. But the war brought one of his best plays, *Heartbreak House* (1917). His description of it as 'a Fantasia in the Russian manner on English themes', is a typically impish mixture of self-assertion and self-deprecation, and there is nothing of Tchekhov's mood of autumnal cadence or of his subtle character-studies. Although it is uneven both in drama and argument, it remains a major intellectual statement about the ineffectuality of the English establishment who have allowed civilization to fall because they have neither the strength nor (in any sense that matters) the will to sustain it. The world belongs to Love, Pride, Heroism and Empire—and Money-making; Shaw later identified characters in *The Simpleton of the Unexpected Isles* explicitly with the first four, but they are here in Hesione, Randall, Hector and Ariadne, while Mangan is the ugly side of Undershaft in *Major Barbara*. Ellie, the 'heroine' of *Heartbreak House*, is a girl of romantic imagination. Act I shows her disillusioned with love, Act II with money. So she turns to the crazy old philosopher, Captain Shotover, who is seeking power by means of mind. He is a character of self-parody and self-criticism, for Shotover has at least been a man of action (as Shaw had not), and in the end his philosophy amounts to rum (which Shaw did not touch). The wisdom of the world has led to war; the wisdom of the philosopher cannot stop it; the dramatic air-raid which ends the play kindles Ellie's romantic imagination afresh, yet deals only death and destruction.

> MR. HUSHABYE:I hope they'll come again tomorrow night.
> ELLIE (*radiant at the prospect*): Oh: I hope so.

It is the most ambiguous ending in all Shaw.

The early years of the twentieth century seem to show a growth in artistic appreciation at the expense of mere antiquarian interest; this at least is a reasonable conclusion from the increased attendance at other galleries combined with a decline in the figure of visitors to the British Museum and the National Gallery. The outbreak of war checked this trend, and the Director of the National Gallery commented on 'the growing interest on the part of the British public in the National Collections, as demonstrated by attendance at the Galleries, the interest shown by the Press and Parliament in the acquisition or presentation of imported pictures, the increasing sensitiveness at the loss of national treasures, and the formation of a powerful and representative society to resist the prevailing exodus.' In 1916 the Government took what Professor Marwick terms the 'incredibly obscurantist decision' to economize by closing all the London museums and galleries. There was vigorous protest, particularly from *The Observer*, *The New Statesman*, *The Nation* and *The Manchester Guardian*, and the Government made a strategic withdrawal. Towards the end of the war the galleries became crowded, and the hunger for aesthetic pleasure, which was to reappear in 1939–45, was evident. Similarly, there was a sellers' market in works of art. In part this was no doubt, as Marwick suggests, due to the affluence of the war profiteers and their desire to be socially accepted; what is important here is that artistic interests were seen as a key to social acceptance.

The Academy continued, under the Presidency of Sir Edward Poynter (1836–1919) the last of the great classicizing painters. War brought changes. Banquets and soirees were discontinued for the duration. The British Red Cross Society moved into the East Wing of Burlington House. The winter exhibition of 1915 featured contemporary painting with a special section of Belgian work: proceeds went to charity. In 1916 the spring exhibition was able to maintain a high standard, but there was no winter exhibition. The following year the winter exhibition consisted of black-and-white work for the first time in Academy history. The exhibition was, in its way, outstanding, but it failed to attract the public.

The work of charity continued. Christie's organized auction sales of paintings for the Red Cross, and brought in £335,000 by them. Some artists, including Sargent, John, Orpen and Muirhead Bone, contributed blank canvases on which they offered to paint a portrait (or a view of a chosen house) for the highest bidder. Hugh Lane actually cabled from America a bid of £10,000 for the Sargent canvas.

For those painters who served in the forces, the war interrupted their work, at least until they were withdrawn to become official war-artists. For others too, like Duncan Grant, alienated from the war, or Ben Nicholson, seriously ill, it was a period of marking time. Edward Wadsworth (1889–1949) was kept busy with naval camouflage which engaged his enthusiasm for the sea and his tendency to geometrical abstraction. Some painters simply continued their pre-war work. The dark theatrical Scot, James Pryde (1866–1941), produced his striking *The Red Ruin* in the middle of the war, yet it is not so much a commentary on war as a view of life, sinister, brilliant and somewhat overplayed. Augustus John (1878–1954) continued painting in all his varied forms. On a major scale, 1916 saw the astonishing *Galway*, a colossal work brilliantly sketched in a single week; later—at the end of the war—he worked on a similar scale in his never fulfilled *Study for a Canadian War Memorial*. Lucien Pissarro (1863–1944) became a British citizen in 1916 after more than a quarter of a century's residence. The closure of the Eragny Press in 1914 effectively ended his work as a creator of artistic books, but a clear, competent impressionism continued to mark his painting, and *Ivy Cottage*,

Coldharbour (1916), a snowmantled landscape with a solitary figure, is as pleasing a work as he ever produced. Sickert (1860–1942) began to decline, and *Ennui* (1913) was almost his last major work, though even in the 1920s genius would very occasionally flash out. During the war, at Chingford and Bath, he showed a great interest in landscape, and used more brilliant colours and light-effects. This was a new departure, but it does not match the work of his Camden Town period. Furthermore, despite his own expressed reservations on the subject, he began increasingly to work from photographs instead of from his own observations and sketches. Roger Fry continued his work with the Omega workshops. He suffered a setback at the outbreak of war, but by 1915 things looked up. As the war dragged on people began to realize that they still had to live somewhere and find furnishings as usual. In 1916 Fry was selling in Norway and Sweden, and even in California. He sold linen and carpets to W. B. Yeats. During the course of his work he faced technical problems over the shape of an umbrella stand, the handle on a dish, the varnish on a bedstead; his friend, the art critic Clive Bell, called him 'a good but impatient craftsman'. One important, and lasting revolution was due to the Omega workshop. In 1917 it featured an exhibition by children from Dudley High School. Their teacher, Miss Richardson, had turned away from the dull, plodding copying of models to free expression. The results revealed considerable creative potential in the children. There was a conservative outcry and an overreaction by radicals who argued for throwing overboard all the traditional technical disciplines. But this quite minor exhibition played its part in turning art education, and art itself, upside down.

New artists were emerging to prominence at this time, simply because their first maturity coincided with the war. Frances Hodgkins (1869–1947) had come from New Zealand via Paris and settled in St Ives for the duration. Here, in 1915, she painted her first oil, the bold but uneven *Two Women with a Basket of Flowers*. The Yorkshireman, Matthew Smith (1879–1959), suddenly in 1916 showed himself to be a major painter with the brilliantly coloured, Fauvist, daring nudes which he called *Fitzroy Street I* and *Fitzroy Street II*. Harold Gilman (1876–1919) painted his undoubted masterpiece, one of the finest British portraits of this century and one of the finest works of the war period, in 1917, *Mrs. Mounter at the Breakfast Table;* the colour is brilliant, and the shimmering surface and broad planes of jug, teapot and cups admirably set off the affectionately perceived features of the delightful, homely woman.

Another painter who produced his greatest work in mid-war was Mark Gertler (1891–1939). Unlike Gilman's work, Gertler's *Merry-go-Round* (1916) is clearly touched by the shadow of war. Indeed, from the outbreak of fighting Gertler seems to have seen human beings as puppets in the grip of mechanical forces, and these inane figures, men and women, soldiers and civilians are carried round and round, endlessly, meaninglessly. D. H. Lawrence saw a photograph of it, and on 9 October he wrote to the artist: 'Your terrible and beautiful picture has just come. This is the finest picture you have ever painted; it is the best modern picture I have seen: I think it is great and true, but it is horrible and terrifying. I'm not sure I wouldn't be too frightened to come and look at the original.'

Richard Nevinson had gone into the war in the Red Cross. In 1915 and 1916 something in him was liberated. He was a journalist, but for the moment he was a journalist of genius. A realist, he portrayed the realism of war, and made it more real by simplification of form and sensible emphasis. His work shows a strong tendency to dehumanize: in *After a Push* no human being is to be seen, but the bare broken trees on the horizon recall the three crosses of a seventeenth century print. As in Nash's *Menin Road*, it is difficult to escape the female symbolism of the hollow shell-holes; it speaks to us of the rape of the earth, and is the most eloquent of all his comments. In *Returning to the Trenches* the break-up of the forms by Cubist techniques depersonalizes the men. *A Motor Ambulance Driver* almost succeeds in suggesting that men and machine have become an undifferentiated whole. The powerfully ironical *La Patrie* shows a first-aid station. The men are lying on stretchers, their faces are masks; our eyes are drawn to the bandages, the bandaged feet, the bandaged head, the bandaged back, the bandaged arm. *La Mitrailleuse* is dominated by the machine-gun and its belt of cartridges, the wire overhead, the wood of the emplacement, the helmets and packs of the soldiers. Their faces, too, are masks. Only as we look searchingly do we realize that there is a dead man among them, for their faces are no less dead than his. Sickert said of his picture that it would 'probably remain the most authoritative and concentrated utterance on the war in the history of painting'. Nevinson was invalided out with rheumatic fever in 1916. He returned as an official war artist, but never matched the concentrated power of his earlier utterance. His soldiers became toy soldiers, rather than dehumanized humans. His work became almost self-parody, or the work of a bumbling disciple. In later years he changed still more and became a pontificating poseur, but for a few months he had shown genius.

Nevinson's vision was prophetic: his art a protest. Muirhead Bone (1876–1953) went out in 1916 however merely to record. Of the two volumes of *The Western Front*, published in 1917, the first had a foreword by Haig: 'The destruction caused by war, the wide areas of devastation, the vast mechanical agencies essential in war, both for transport and the offensive, the masses of supplies required, and the wonderful cheerfulness and indomitable courage of the soldiers under varying climatic conditions, are worthy subjects for the artist who aims at recording for all time the spirit of the age in which he has lived.' But this is not quite what Bone does. There is little in these volumes to foster the romance of heroism; little, either, of the revulsion which Nevinson showed. Bone was a consummate craftsman, no more, no less. He records; he does not interpret. His soldiers are not filmstars or dehumanized instruments of the war-machine, but very ordinary people caught where he happened to see them, climbing a ladder or asleep on deck, or mending a puncture. The ruins of Ypres move us no more and no less than Amiens in its glory, with the only sign of war in patrolling aircraft. The work of greater artists may be uneven because it depends on vision and inspiration, which may grow dull and clogged. Bone's work is even in temper and quality. for that reason he is at his most effective in portraying the machine, and his drawings of tanks, or of the work of a gun factory, are an accurate record of aspects of war which others neglected.

Photography was also available for recording the war, and the collection in the Imperial War Museum forms an impressive record. There is a remarkable picture by an unknown photographer showing Château Wood, Ypres. Four privates check as they trudge, in a sort of ordered march, across duckboards spanning a lake of water and mud. In the foreground a tree has snapped and is lying like some monstrous railway signal alongside the track. In the background gaunt skeletons of trees stretch like an army of the dead into the mist. It is as evocative as Nevinson or Nash. But the main development in

British photography was dissociated from the war. Alvin Langdon Coburn, an American photographer, had already in 1913 maintained that a photographer had as much right as a Cubist painter to manipulate perspective. In 1916 he called for an exhibition of abstract photography. He himself was producing 'vortographs' taken by a camera through a prismatic complex of mirrors, transmuting a concrete subject into pictorial patterns. One of these was published in *Photograms of the Year* for 1917: one reviewer amused himself by wondering which way up it looked best. An exhibition of his work, which included bird's-eye views of New York, was held in London in 1917; Pound (who, with Wyndham Lewis, thoroughly approved) wrote the introduction to the catalogue, declaring that these photographs reflected the basic principles of Vorticism and represented the coming aesthetic; Coburn himself asked 'Why should not the camera artist break away from the worn-out conventions that, even in its comparatively short existence, have begun to cramp and restrict his medium?'

The cartoonists of those days produced little of any lasting worth, being too self-righteous in their indignation. Max Beerbohm, who might have penetrated deeper, chose rather to retire from the scene.

The anti-German propaganda can be seen in the pages of *Punch*. Perhaps its most interesting expression was Frank Reynolds's well known cartoon *Study of a Prussian Household having its Morning Hate*. There they are; the father, paunchy and heavy-jowled, leaning on table, fist clenched; the mother, leaning comfortably back in her chair to enjoy a reposeful hate; the grown-up daughter, standing and attitudinizing; the next youngest brooding in hostile meditation; the youngest of all working herself up into a frenzy of hatred; and the delightfully frowning dachshund. It is technically brilliant: see for example how the horizontal hatchments bring out the rotundity of the parents. Yet one wonders now just what emotion it was intended to elicit. Was it meant to arouse hostility? Or to suggest that the Germans were not to be taken seriously?

The great political cartoonists of the war were the Dutchman Louis Raemaeker, the Australian Will Dyson, and, on the other side of the lines, George Grosz. Only one English cartoonist made a name for good humour without political satire. This was Captain Bruce Bairnsfather (1888–1959) who created in Old Bill an admirable type

75

of the British Tommy, grumbling or cheerful, in simplified but authentic surroundings. One of Bairnsfather's most famous pictures shows a nervous soldier sheltering in a shell hole, as explosions burst all round, with an old hand who is saying to him 'Well, if you knows of a better 'ole, go to it.' Wyndham Lewis once said that Old Bill was the true hero of the war and won the war.

Ireland was relatively sheltered from the war, but not from its own tragedy of violence, and sensitive artists could not fail to be affected by what was going on around them. Arnold Bax (1883–1953) was not really Irish at all, but had absorbed a great deal of Celtic romanticism. We can sense something of the background of war in his *Second Violin Sonata* (1915) with its remote harmonies associated with the appearance of Death as 'the grey dancer in the twilight', but the best-known of all his works, *Tintagel* (1917) seems more of an escape into nature and the sea in all its moods. Most of his wartime compositions are escapist in mood, although his *First Symphony* (1921–2) perhaps contains his mature reflections on the war. Bax himself called it 'oppresive and catastrophic'. Even on 19 May 1918 the lines he wrote in Harriet Cohen's autograph album only allude to 'churlish circumstances':

> This for the maiden with the daffodil
> Whose fingers' intricate enchantments fill
> Our ears with far-strayed echoes of Romance.
>   Let us forget all churlish circumstance
> And gather aught we may have said or sung
>   Of life's most honourably remembered days,
> And while dreams burn and she is fair and young
>   Bring her each one his meed of love and praise.

(Scott-Sutherland p.49)

(He had in 1915 written a piano piece 'The Maiden with the Daffodil') Bax himself was not deeply identified with the Irish cause in the uprising of Easter 1916, but some of his friends were, and he wrote *An Irish Elegy* (later called *In Memoriam*) for Padraic Pearse. It is a haunting, controlled piece, in a single movement for cor anglais, harp and string quartet. Bax's poem 'In Glencullen' (written under his pen name of Dermot O'Byrne) expresses more brutally the anguish that Easter:

You can leave your slane to rust, old man
And stretch all day in bed;
No more I'll rinse out crock and pan,
Or soak the flour for bread;
But think my fill of Mount Jerome
And a heap of nettles far from home
Where Dan lies stiff and dead.

But first I'll burn the creepy-stool
His little naked feet
Would dangle round and him from school;
(O! nice they were and neat!)
Yon creepy's pain that's fit to fill
Since Dan went whistling down the hill
To die in Sackville Street.

It was W. B. Yeats (1865–1939) who was supremely equipped to express the agony of Ireland. He had passed from sentimental evocation of the mythical past to a satirical treatment of the contemporary scene; he had pruned the luxuriance of his language and disciplined his imagery. Now he succeeded in focusing all his controlled imagination on to the tragedy of 1916.

I have met them at close of day
Coming with vivid faces
From counter or desk among grey
Eighteenth century houses.
I have passed with a nod of the head
Or polite meaningless words,
Or have lingered awhile and said
Polite meaningless words,
And thought before I had done
Of a mocking tale or a gibe
To please a companion
Around the fire at the club,
Being certain that they and I
But lived where motley is worn:
All changed, changed utterly;
A terrible beauty is born.

Yeats did a rare thing; he succeeded in shaping a contemporary myth. Pearse and Connolly became mythical symbols as well as people. He did not idealize or sentimentalize; he called one of the dead men 'a drunken vainglorious lout'. He did not support their violence. But he saw that their execution transformed their world and his, and expressed the fact with studied power.

4

Finale and Aftermath

THE winter of 1916–17 was bitingly cold. When spring came, it served only to thaw the ground enough to flood the trenches with nearly-freezing water. Little wonder it marked a growth of bitterness towards the progress of the war. No longer could it be seen as a passing incident to be entered with gay abandon and forgotten; the fear was that it would never end. Those in power at home patronized the soldiers who in their turn began to hate those in power at home. They saw themselves increasingly as victims of the system, as sufferers in a conflict of the generations in which the old sat comfortably at home, and sent out the young to die. Idealists had seen their idealism knocked away, blasted and shattered. The Tommies had no illusions to shatter: they were merely fed up.

The Germans withdrew to the newly defined Hindenburg Line early in 1917. In March impatience with the government in Russia and its inefficient conduct of the war led to the fall of the monarchy, and later in the year gave the Bolsheviks their chance. It was twelve months before the peace treaty with Germany was signed at Brest Litovsk. In April the Allies recaptured Vimy Ridge, but at such cost that there were mutinies in the French army. The second half of the year saw the terrible, futile slaughter of Passchendaele; British losses alone were 324,000. Meantime the Germans, who had withdrawn from their U-boat campaign after the sinking of the *Lusitania*, renewed it again, and in April 1917 nearly two hundred British ships were lost. But this renewed campaign brought the US into the war, and that was to be crucial to the Allies' eventual victory.

On 21 March 1918 Ludendorff, helped by heavy fog, made a surprise attack on the Somme. He blew a hole in the British lines, and advanced forty miles in a few days. The Allies seemed to be falling apart. The situation was desperate. Haig issued his 'backs to the wall' message: 'Many of us now are tired. To those I would say that victory belongs to the side which holds out the longest.' In England the people were so restive that the government were actually ready to offer Bottomley, who professed to be 'the soldier's friend', a place in the cabinet. Then four things saved the Allies: Ludendorff's failure to consolidate his gains or achieve a decisive breakthrough; Lloyd George's vigour; Allenby's victories in the East; and, most importantly, the arrival of more American troops. The German offensive spent itself and counter-attacks pushed them back; the fleet mutinied and revolution spread to the cities; on 9 November the Kaiser abdicated and on 11 November the armistice was signed. The troops were dazed; they could hardly recognize the peace. In London people went wild; they commandeered omnibuses and careered around in them, kissed strangers in the streets and lit a bonfire at the foot of Nelson's column. It had been a damned close-run thing.

Some hope for the future there was, some candles flickering in the darkness. Internationally, the idea of a League of Nations was on the way to becoming a reality. At home the Imperial War Conference of 1917 recognized that the Dominions and India could not remain in their present dependent status after the war. Details of 'the read-justment of the constitutional relations of the component parts of the Empire' were postponed, but the principle that the Dominions should be recognized as autonomous nations of an Imperial Commonwealth laid down; the attitude towards India was more ambiguous, but the progressive 'Indianization' of the administration was accepted as a means to the 'realization of responsible government in India as an integral part of the British Empire'. In the same year of 1917 the Whitley Committee moved towards the establishment of Joint Councils of employers and workers to improve Industrial Relations. In 1918 H. A. L. Fisher promoted his Education Act, raising the school leaving age to fourteen; he established free places at secondary school for the intellectually abler; he also standardized teachers' salaries and improved their conditions of service. In June 1918 the Representation of the People Act passed smoothly through Parliament. It gave voting rights to more additional people than all previous acts put together, including six million women, and except for the University seats and business premises, it accepted the principle 'One man one vote'; but it disfranchised conscientious objectors for five years.

On the other hand, there were serious problems facing Britain at the end of the war. Her economic outlook was grim. The British Government had financed its allies to the extent of £1,825,000,000 and to do this had borrowed over £1,000,000,000 from the US. The loans were assumed to be solid assets, which they were not; the borrowing proved a solid debit. There was something in Bernard Partridge's cartoon which showed the nations writing IOU on one another's backs till at the end of the line John Bull writes IPAYU on Uncle Sam. Politically there was a large question-mark against Ireland. The executions of 1916 had only exacerbated the situation. Sinn Fein was sweeping the country and with the breakdown of the Dublin Convention early in 1918 any hope of a peaceable solution dimmed and faded. Also there was growing uncertainty about the unprincipled Lloyd George. Could he be trusted? Could he fulfil the promises of peace? Could he even hold the country together? The answer, in the event, was No. Sassoon recorded bitterly how the grey men emerged from their shelters and took over again. Above all, Britain had to face the loss of the best part of a generation.

Henri Barbusse's remarkable novel *Le Feu*, a protest against the war in the name of humanity, had appeared as early as 1916; in 1917 it was translated into English as *Under Fire*. It had a major effect on the two leading English poets of the last period of the war.

The lesser of the two as a poet, Siegfried Sassoon (1886–1967), had been a volunteer at the beginning of the war, before Rupert Brooke, for example, was involved. He was naive and idealistic:

> The anguish of the earth absolves our eyes
> Till beauty shines in all that we can see.
> War is our scourge: yet war has made us wise,
> And fighting for our freedom, we are free.

His view, as Robert Graves recalled, was simplistic. His gallantry was undoubted, he was awarded the Military Cross for it. But something else was nagging within him. Graves wrote understandingly that 'the direction of Siegfried's unconquerable idealism changed with his environment; he varied between happy warrior and bitter pacifist.' In 1916 he had been on sick leave in Blighty. In 1917 he returned to France, fought in the battle of Arras and was wounded. In May of

81

that year he published *The Old Huntsman*, a volume of verse, including 'Absolution' from which the lines above are taken, and 'Blighters', one of his most powerful pieces of realism:

> The House is crammed: tier beyond tier they grin
> And cackle at the show, while prancing ranks
> Of harlots shrill the chorus, drunk with din;
> 'We're sure the Kaiser loves our dear old Tanks!'

> I'd like to see a Tank come down the stalls,
> Lurching to rag-time tunes, or 'Home, sweet Home',
> And there'd be no more jokes in Music-halls
> To mock the riddled corpses round Bapaume.

Epigrammatic poems are not difficult to sustain for someone with a sense of words, but this is highly skilled. There are two superimposed pictures: the music-hall at Liverpool, and the realities of the Front. The chorus-girls, like the soldiers, are in ranks. They prance like outmoded cavalry on parade. The tank lurches, but whereas it is the real thing, they are only playing. The enjambement of the first stanza contrasts with the relentlessly end-stopped onset of the second. Ironically, *Home, sweet Home* was a song the soldiers loved to hear. The poem is structured around strong, blatant rhymes, and held together by carefully placed initial letters, crammed-cackle-chorus-corpses-Kaiser, show-shrill, tank-tunes, rag-time-riddled; only at drunk-din is alliteration allowed to obtrude. The language is utterly, unmistakably clear. The final word, Bapaume, gives the whole poem a strong sense of reality in a precise geographical location. It is a device which Sassoon liked to use.

Sassoon refused to go on:

I am making this statement as an act of wilful defiance of military authority, because I believe that the War is being deliberately prolonged by those who have the power to end it. I am a soldier, convinced that I am acting on behalf of soldiers. I believe that this war, upon which I entered as a war of defence and liberation, has now become a war of aggression and conquest. I believe that the purposes for which I and my fellow soldiers entered upon this War should have been so clearly stated as to have made it impossible to change them, and that, had this been done, the objects which actuated us would now be attainable by negotiation. I have seen and endured the sufferings of the troops, and I can no longer be a party to prolong these sufferings for ends which I believe to be evil and unjust. I am not protesting against the conduct of the War, but against the political errors and insincerities for which the fighting men are being sacrificed. On behalf of those who are suffering now I make this protest against the deception which is being practised on them; also I believe that I may help to destroy the callous complacency with which the majority of those at home regard the continuance of agonies which they do not share, and which they have not sufficient imagination to realize.

The statement is taken from *Memories of an Infantry Officer*, where the events are fictionalized, but the situation was real . . . Sassoon risked court-martial, but the authorities evaded this by declaring him a victim of shell-shock and tucking him up in hospital. In 1918 he published another, even more bitter, volume of verse entitled *Counter-Attack*. The note of idealism was wholly gone. Typical is 'The General'.

> 'Good-morning; good-morning!' the General said
> When we met him last week on our way to the line.
> Now the soldiers he smiled at most of 'em dead,
> And we're cursing his staff for incompetent swine.
> 'He's a cheery old card', grunted Harry to Jack
> As they slogged up to Arras with rifle and pack
>
>   *   *   *   *
>
> But he did for them both by his plan of attack.

This is not as good as 'Blighters'; the third and fourth lines spoil the impact of the last. But it has power. The simple repetition 'Good-morning; good-morning!' creates a character, a living person. The single word Arras, as Bapaume did in 'Blighters', produces an instant realism. The unexpected triple rhyme points the last line. Another poem 'They', is an attack on a compromising church and its facile spokesman.

> The Bishop tells us: 'When the boys come back
> 'They will not be the same; for they'll have fought
> 'In a just cause: they lead the last attack
> 'On Anti-Christ; their comrades' blood has bought
> 'New right to breed on honourable race,
> 'They have challenged Death and dared him face to face.'
>
> 'We're none of us the same!' the boys reply.
> 'For George lost both his legs; and Bill's stone blind;
> 'Poor Jim's shot through the lungs and like to die;
> 'And Bert's gone syphilitic: you'll not find
> 'A chap who's served that hasn't found some change.'
> And the Bishop said: 'The ways of God are strange!'

The point is made, and made legitimately. But it is very strident. No more strident, though, than the defenders of the war. It is the note of urgency which gives it power. He wrote, however, one poem of hope. It is familiar to thousands who do not know its origin. He was watching a regiment on the march in the grimmest period of the war. Suddenly, spontaneously, they burst into song:

> Everyone suddenly burst out singing;
> And I was filled with such delight
> As prisoned birds must find in freedom,
> Winging wildly across the white
> Orchards and dark-green fields; on—on—and out of sight,
>
> Everyone's voice was suddenly lifted;
> And beauty came like the setting sun:
> My heart was shaken with tears; and horror
> Drifted away . . . O, but everyone
> Was a bird; and the song was wordless; the singing will never be done.

Sassoon's anti-war poetry found an unexpected admirer in Winston Churchill, who had many of the poems by heart.

Sassoon, as well as Barbusse, influenced Wilfred Owen (1893–1918) who is now seen as a major poet. Owen, whose parents were Welsh, grew up in Shropshire. A lonely boy, nicknamed the wolf, Owen had, from his youth, had ambitions to be a great poet. When the war broke out he did not, like Sassoon, promptly volunteer, and it was a year or more before he eventually applied for a commission in the Artists' Rifles. He hated war, but he never followed Sassoon in standing aside from it; he described himself as 'a conscientious objector with a very seared conscience'. He knew that he was called to turn the other cheek, but kept saying 'Vengeance is mine, I, Owen will repay.' He hated army life, but despite his shyness he became a diligent officer. In 1917 he went to France and was sent back shell-shocked, and it was more than a year before he was fit to return to France.

It was during this period of 1917–1918 that he met Sassoon; during this period, too, he wrote his finest poems. The mood of protest was heavy upon him: if he heard people talk lightly of the glory of war, he would produce photographs of hideously wounded men and say quietly 'I think these might interest you.' But he went back to the front. Edmund Blunden said that he could not help

24. *A Vortograph*, Alvin Langdon Coburn, *c.* 1917

25. *Aerial View of Passchendaele, Before Battle,* 1917

26. *Aerial View of Passchendaele, After Battle,* 1917

27. *Chateau Wood, Ypres,* 29th October 1917

28. *Edward Elgar*, 1911

29. *Isaac Rosenberg*, Self Portrait

30. *Edward Thomas*, J. Wheatley, 1915

31. *Ezra Pound*, Henri Gaudier Brzeska

32. *D. H. Lawrence*, Ian Juta

33. *Siegfried Sassoon*, Glyn Philpot, 1917

34. *Roger Fry*, Self Portrait

35. *Sir Frank Benson*, R. G. Eves

36. *Lytton Strachey*, N. Hamnett

37. *Edith Sitwell*, Wyndham Lewis

38. *Rupert Brooke*, Clara Ewald, 1911

39. *Wilfred Owen*   40. *Clara Butt*

41. *Augustus John*, 1917

2. *T. E. Lawrence*, Augustus John

43. *Your Country Needs You*, Alfred Leete, 1914

44. *Take up the Sword of Justice*, Sir Bernard Partridge

45. *Remember Scarborough*, Anon

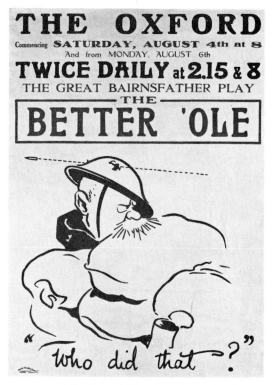

47. *The Better 'Ole*, Playbill, Oxford

46. *The Better 'Ole*, Playbill, Hull, 1917

48. *It is Far Better to Face the Bullets*, Anon

BACK·HIM·UP BUY WAR BONDS

49. *Buy War Bonds*,
Frank Brangwyn

THE ZEPPELIN RAIDS : THE VOW OF VENGEANCE
Drawn for 'The Daily Chronicle' by Frank Brangwyn ARA

'DAILY CHRONICLE' READERS ARE
COVERED AGAINST THE RISKS OF
BOMBARDMENT BY ZEPPELIN OR
═══ AEROPLANE ═══

50. *The Zeppelin Raids*,
Frank Brangwyn

51. Cover of *Evelyn Hastings*, Victoria Cross

52. *Study of a Prussian Household having its Morning Hate*, F. Reynolds, *Punch*, Feb. 24, 1915

The Dead.

These hearts were woven of human joys and cares,
  Washed marvellously with sorrow, swift to mirth.
The years had given them kindness. Dawn was theirs,
  And sunset, & the colours of the earth.
These had seen movement and heard music; known
  Slumber & waking; loved; gone proudly friended;
Felt the quick stir of wonder; sat alone;
  Touched flowers & furs & cheeks. And this is ended.

There are waters, blown by changing winds to laughter
and lit by the rich skies, all day. And after,
Frost, with a gesture, stays the waves that dance
And wandering loveliness. He leaves a white
Unbroken glory, a gathered radiance,
A width, a shining peace, under the night.

R.B.

53. Original *MS of The Dead*, Rupert Brooke

himself and added, with an allusion to Owen's favourite poet, Keats:
'He was one of those to whom the miseries of the world are misery
and will not let them rest, and he went back to spend his life in doing
what he could to palliate them.' Owen was killed in November 1918,
just a week before the Armistice.

He had been planning a collection of his poetry, and left an
unfinished preface.

This book is not about heroes. English poetry is not yet fit to speak of them
   Nor is it about deeds, or lands, nor anything about glory, honour, might,
majesty, dominion or power, except War.
   Above all I am not concerned with Poetry.
   My subject is War, and the pity of War.
   The Poetry is in the pity.
   Yet these elegies are to this generation in no sense consolatory. They may
be to the next. All a poet can do today is warn. That is why the true Poets
must be truthful.
   (If I thought the letter of this book would last, I might have used proper
names; but if the spirit of it survives—survives Prussia—my ambition and
those names will have achieved themselves fresher fields than Flanders. . . .)

'The Poetry is in the pity.' It has been much quoted, but of Owen it
is true: he is, in the right sense, a pitiful poet, and this is the impulse
behind his writing. Sassoon said of him 'In a young man of twenty-
four his selflessness was extraordinary. the clue to his poetic genius
was sympathy, not only in his detached outlook upon humanity but
in all his actions and responses towards individuals.' He matched to
this a technique of half-rhymes which expresses well the ambiguities
of his position. We find it even in the 1917 poems, such as the closely
observed, sensitive, honest 'Exposure':

   Our brains ache, in the merciless iced east winds that knive us. . . .
   Wearied we keep awake because the night is silent. . . .
   Low drooping flares confuse our memory of the salient. . . .
   Worried by silence, sentries whisper, curious, nervous,
      But nothing happens.

In contrast to Grenfell's 'Into Battle,' which hymns the glory of
action, Owen writes of passively waiting. The technique is not per-
fected, but even in the early stages it has power: note the internal
'iced east' as well as the final syllables, and the effect of the shorter
unrhymed last line. The device is seen at its finest in 'Strange

Meeting'; Blunden said of this poem that 'again and again by means of it he creates remoteness, darkness, emptiness, shock, echo, the last word'.

It seemed that out of battle I escaped
Down some profound dull tunnel, long since scooped
Through granites which titanic wars had groined.
Yet also there encumbered sleepers groaned,
Too fast in thought or death to be bestirred,
Then, as I probed them, one sprang up, and stared
With piteous recognition in fixed eyes,
Lifting distressful hands as if to bless
And by his smile, I knew that sullen hall,
By his dead smile I knew we stood in Hell.
With a thousand pains that vision's face was grained;
Yet no blood reached there from the upper ground,
And no guns thumped, or down the flues made moan.
'Strange friend', I said, 'here is no cause to mourn.'
'None', said that other, 'save the undone years,
The hopelessness. Whatever hope is yours,
Was my life also; I went hunting wild
After the wildest beauty in the world,
Which lies not calm in eyes, or braided hair,
But mocks the steady running of the hour,
And if it grieves, grieves richlier than here.
For of my glee might many men have laughed,
And of my weeping something had been left,
Which must die now. I mean the truth untold,
The pity of war, the pity war distilled.
Now men will go content with what we spoiled,
Or, discontent, boil bloody, and be spilled.
They will be swift with swiftness of the tigress.
None will break ranks, though nations trek from progress.
Courage was mine, and I had mystery,
Wisdom was mine, and I had mastery:
To miss the march of this retreating world
Into vain citadels that are not walled.
Then, when much blood had clogged their chariot-wheels,
I would go up and wash them from sweet wells,
Even with truths that lie too deep for taint.
I would have poured my spirit without stint
But not through wounds; not on the cess of war.

Foreheads of men have bled where no wounds were.
I am the enemy you killed, my friend.
I knew you in this dark: for so you frowned
Yesterday through me as you jabbed and killed.
I parried; but my hands were loath and cold.
Let us sleep now . . .'

In 1917 Owen wrote home: 'I have comprehended a light which never will filter into the dogma of any national church: namely that one of Christ's essential commands was: Passivity at any price! . . . Christ is literally in No Man's Land. There men often hear his voice: Greater love hath no man than this, that a man lay down his life—for a friend. Is it spoken in English only and French? I do not believe so. Thus you see how pure Christianity will not fit in with pure patriotism . . . Christians have deliberately cut some of the main teachings of their code.' In that letter Owen takes a text which was to be mouthed emotively from hundreds of pulpits on successive Armistice Days, and saw what the preachers failed to see—that Christ talked of laying down life freely for a friend, not compulsorily for a state. (Charles Sims had painted an almost blasphemous allegory on this text, a Tommy crucified with wife and children and aged parents around him, in 1917.) Owen saw that happen time and again in No Man's Land, which is why he stayed in the army. The letter represents a kind of conversion, for though his mother had planned the Christian ministry for him, he had become an agnostic. Although he turned to the Christ he did not turn to the church. It is worth looking at one of his weaker poems 'At a Calvary near the Ancre'.

One ever hangs where shelled roads part,
  In this war He too lost a limb,
But his disciples hide apart,
  And now the Soldiers bear with Him.

Near Golgotha strolls many a priest,
  And in their faces there is pride
That they were flesh-marked by the Beast
  By whom the gentle Christ's denied.

The scribes on all the people shove
  And bawl allegiance to the state,
But they who love the greater love
  Lay down their life; they do not hate.

Here the rhyming is straight: part-apart is weak. The syntax is contorted: look at the first line of the final stanza. The rhythmic structure is too weak. The language borders on cliché. Yet there is power. The poem can be compared with Sassoon's 'They'; the theme, the apostasy of the representatives of Christ, is the same, but Owen feels it more deeply. Sassoon puts his bishop up against the results of war he has not faced. Owen puts his priest up against a Christ-figure who has been crucified and shelled, and against common soldiers who have retained an element of love. Of course there is an element of sentimentalism: the soldier's job is to kill, not to die. But whereas Owen's values are personal, Sassoon is fighting for a cause. One last example of Owen's poetry may be taken in his most delicate poem, 'Futility':

> Move him into the sun—
> Gently its touch awoke him once,
> At home, whispering of fields unsown.
> Always it woke him, even in France,
> Until this morning and this snow.
> If anything might rouse him now
> The kind old sun will know.
>
> Think how it wakes the seeds,—
> Woke, once, the clays of a cold star.
> Are limbs, so dear-achieved, are sides,
> Full-nerved—still warm—too hard to stir?
> Was it for this the clay grew tall?
> —O what made fatuous sunbeams toil
> To break earth's sleep at all?

Here the pararhymes are effectively mixed in the triplet with a devastatingly final true rhyme. The simplicity of the first line, the use of monosyllables in the last line of each stanza and especially in 'Was it for this the clay grew tall?', the climactic 'fatuous', the linking of man with nature, the economy of statement, the reticent absence of any reference to the war except the one word France (compare Sassoon's use of Bapaume and Arras), the pity, all add up to one of the greater short poems in the English language.

The mood of Sassoon and Owen is found in many of the contributions to *Wheels*, whose cycles were turned by Edith, Osbert and Sacheverell Sitwell. They saw what was happening before most other people. The first issue actually appeared in 1916: *The Pall Mall Gazette* described it as 'conceived in morbid eccentricity and executed in fierce factitious gloom'. The poems conveyed the realism, not the romance of warfare. E. Wyndham Tennant's 'The Mad Soldier' is a typical example:

> Can't you see
> When the flare goes up? Ssh! boys; what's that noise?
> Do you know what these rats eat? Body-meat.

The harsh assonances and the insistent monosyllables set off the climactic word. Tennant was killed a few weeks after writing these words. Osbert Sitwell was particularly bitter about those who sat at home. In 'Armchair' he expresses the musings of a patriot of the older generation:

> That day I'ld send my grandsons out to France
> And wish I'ld got ten other ones to send
> (One cannot sacrifice too much I'ld say)

It is very mordant. *Wheels* is important because it offered an alternative form of expression to Marsh's Georgians. The Sitwells themselves wrote a kind of anti-representational poetry, a literary equivalent to Picasso's Cubism: even the cover-design, which started in the form of traditional satire, moved to modernistic art.

As we look back with hindsight, we can see a turning-point in English poetry in a slim volume published in 1917 by a young American and entitled *Prufrock and other Observations*. T. S. Eliot (1888–1965) already, in 1917, showed a meticulous control of form, however free that form might seem to be, a capacity for coining memorable phrases, a probing into the shams of life and exposing the discrepancy between appearance and reality, a readiness to see gravity in levity and levity in gravity. 'The Love Song of J. Alfred Prufrock' had in fact been published in 1915. The scene is banal, a confrontation at teatime in a down-at-heel section of the town with the fog outside, while

> In the room the women come and go
> Talking of Michelangelo.

Much of Eliot's art consists in such juxtapositions.

> I grow old . . . I grow old. . . .
> I shall wear the bottoms of my trousers rolled.

Shall I part my hair behind? Do I dare to eat a peach?
I shall wear white flannel trousers, and walk upon the beach.
I have heard the mermaids singing, each to each.

The mermaids were part of the traditional equipage of poetry, but not the rolled trouser-bottoms. So in 'Preludes' we encounter 'smells of steaks in passageways' and 'the burnt-out ends of smoky days'. 'Rhapsody on a Windy Night' focuses on a street-lamp, and we see a gutter-cat devouring a morsel of rancid butter. A mischievous portrait of Bertrand Russell as 'Mr. Apollinax' shows his priapean propensities and his tinkling laughter 'like an irresponsible foetus'. Only in the exquisite 'La Figlia che Piange' is the traditional lyric note unblurred; its movement of mood is extraordinarily subtle; its cynicism delicately expressed:

I should find
Some way incomparably light and deft,
Some way we both should understand,
Simple and faithless as a smile and a shake of the hand.

This is not war poetry. It is poetry of an empty, purposeless world which has made war possible. It conveys, in Pound's description of Prufrock, 'the quintessence of futility'. It provided the perfect instrument for expressing the waste-land of post-war disillusion.

In *The Criterion* for July 1932 Ezra Pound looked back on the war period, and associated his development with that of Eliot, who 'displayed great tact, or enjoyed good fortune, in arriving in London at a particular date with a formed style of his own. He also participated in a movement to which no name has even been given. That is to say, at a particular date in a particular room, two authors, neither engaged in picking the other's pocket, decided that the dilutation of *vers libre*, Amygism, Lee Masterism, general floppiness had gone too far and that some counter-current must be set going. Parallel situation centuries ago in China. Remedy prescribed "Emaux et Camées" or the Bay State Hymn Book. Rhyme and regular strophes.'

Pound specified *Prufrock* (1917) and his own *Hugh Selwyn Mauberley* (1920) as coming from this decision. (The references are to Amy Lowell's development of Imagism, Lee Masters's *Spoon River Anthology* and Théophile Gautier's renunciation of romantic expansion for ironic concision). *Mauberley*, in fact, itself reflected something of the war.

There died a myriad,
And of the best, among them,
For an old bitch, gone in the teeth,
For a botched civilization,

Charm, smiling at the good mouth,
Quick eyes gone under earth's lid,

For two gross of broken statues,
For a few thousand battered books.

By 1920 Pound felt that the civilization for which the war should have been fought had been degraded. He left London, and continued to live without roots on the continent.

Another major stride in the future was taken in 1918 when Bridges finally let the public see the poetry of Gerard Manley Hopkins (1844–1889). Hopkins might have seemed a voice from the past, but he struck the ear like a voice from the future. With Hopkins, as Michael Roberts excellently put it, 'the problem which is his today is the world's tomorrow'. His is a poetry of conflict, of crisis, and he found the way to express this in complex new-minted words, contorted syntax, intense alliteration, strongly pulsating original rhythms:

Million-fuelèd, / nature's bonfire burns on.
But quench her bonniest, dearest / to her, her clearest-selvèd spark
Man, how fast his firedint, / his mark on mind, is gone!
Both are in an unfathomable, all is in an enormous dark
Drowned. O pity and indig / nation! Manshape, that shone
Sheer off, disseveral, a star, / death blots black out, nor mark
        Is any of him at all so stark
But vastness blurs and time / beats level. .

It might have been written in 1918 as a commentary on the war, rather than thirty years earlier; none of the war poets, not even Owen, had the equipment with which to express the underlying pattern so powerfully. It was to speak with increasing authority to those who in the coming years felt the continuing crisis and were searching for a point of creative faith.

G. K. Chesterton, as he had a bad time at the beginning of the war, had an equally bad time at its conclusion. In September 1916 his brother Cecil joined the East Surreys as a private, and GKC took over the editorship of *The New Witness*. The editor's chair was never the best outlet for his particular gifts, and his work has a sense of brotherly duty about it. Cecil was fatally wounded in the last weeks of fighting, and died in hospital on 6 December, 1918. His brother wrote 'He lived long enough to march to the victory which was for him a supreme vision of liberty and the light. The work which he put second, but very near to the other, he left for us to do. There are many of us who will abandon many other things, and recognize no greater duty than to do it.' He saw Lloyd George and Rufus Isaacs, men he believed to have been implicated in the Marconi scandal, leading the peace delegation. He wrote, with a bitterness alien to his nature, his 'Elegy in a Country churchyard'.

> The men that worked for England
> They have their graves at home:
> And bees and birds of England
> About the cross can roam.
>
> But they that fought for England,
> Following a falling star,
> Alas, alas for England
> They have their graves afar.
>
> And they that rule in England,
> In stately conclave met,
> Alas, alas for England
> They have no graves as yet.

He wrote, even as he sorrowed for his brother, an open letter to Isaacs, now Lord Reading, who would, he believed, represent the interests of international finance at Versailles, and in those interests sacrifice Poland and bolster up Prussia. And he asserted, time and again, that the armistice marked a long truce, not a peace.

H. G. Wells, on the other hand, was in one of his elements in the *persona* of the Reformer. Here was a unique chance to build a new world; the words sound tawdry now, but then they were as fresh-minted gold. As early as May 1917 he had written a letter to *The Times*, which the editor rejected, advocating a universal League of Free Nations, controlling the armed power of the world; Britain would give up empire, navy and monarchy. He now saw in the League of Nations something of his New Republic, his World State. Only gradually did he discern that what had emerged was but 'the simulacrum of peace'. He turned to the work of the intellect. His pamphlet *History is One* was widely read. He pressed the League to the writing of the sort of international history which Unesco has at last sponsored. There was no one to do it but himself and in an incredibly short space of time *The Outline of History* appeared. It was hasty and uneven, sometimes unscholarly; and there can always be dispute whether he identified the right peaks. But it was, and is, lucid and exciting, and valuable in the stress on interdependence; he came to see it as an essay on the growth of association. It met the hopes of the armistice as *Mr. Britling* had met the hopes of 1916. Wells's greatest work was his creation of Kipps, Mr. Polly and Mr. Lewisham; next were the prophetic scientific romances. We may regret that those veins of inspiration became exhausted. But there is a sense in which if he had not had the sort of mind which became absorbed by the concept of a World Brain, nothing lasting would have sprung from him at any time.

Shaw had used the period of the war to work on which was designed to be his masterpiece, *Back to Methuselah*. On 25 July, 1918 we find him saying 'I have written a play with intervals of thousands of years (in the future) between the acts; but now I find I must make each act into a full-length play.' The result was not the intended masterpiece. Its length is inappropriate to the medium; it is sprawling and diffuse and the Ancients are merely tedious. Hesketh Pearson commented that if long-livers make nothing more exhilarating of life than Shaw's Ancients, 'there will still be a strong argument in favour of pole-axing everybody at the age of fifty'. But there are many brilliances in *Back to Methuselah*: the second act of the Adam and Eve sequence, and Adam's uneasiness before the prospect of immortality; the delightfully entertaining parodies of Asquith and Lloyd George in 'The Gospel of the Brothers Barnabas'; the despondent beauty of 'As Far as Thoughts can Reach'. All through there is vigorous thought, and sparkling language—but it does not add up to a successful drama. Despite the thought and writing, *Back to Methuselah* has some claim to being Shaw's least successful achievement in theatrical terms. What it does achieve, especially when considered together with its preface, is a really remarkable exploration of the implications of evolutionary theory. J. D. Bernal said once that the preface should form a part of every biological student's education becuse it sees Darwinism in its social context. Shaw was a disciple of Samuel Butler, who said that Dar-

93

win's doctrine of natural selection 'banished mind from the universe'. In the debate between Vitalists and Mechanists, Shaw is on the side of the Vitalists. The preface is a defence of Creative Evolution, just as the play is an account of how it might operate. In a curious way, therefore, just as Wells came out of the war with a vision of a new world backed by a religious mystique, so did Shaw. But it takes a sharper theology than Shaw's to make drama out of a panorama extending from creation to fulfilment. Part II, 'The Gospel of the Brothers Barnabas', reflects the war as it shows the works of the Sons of Cain. 'To me the awful thing about their political incompetence was that they had to kill their own sons.'

Among the iconoclasms of the end of the war was Lytton Strachey's *Eminent Victorians* (1918). Strachey (1880-1932), one of the Bloomsbury group, and a friend of Roger Fry, had written an unmemorable *Landmarks in French Literature*. He was a pacifist and a conscientious objector. At his tribunal in May 1916 they asked him 'What would you do if you saw a German soldier trying to rape your sister?' He replied fastidiously 'I should try to get between them.' Now he set himself to debunk the heroes of the broken world. His mood, and indeed his weapons, were those of Macaulay (when his hostility was stirred) or Gibbon, but he operated on a smaller scale, and his knife gives the impression of being that much sharper. Cardinal Manning, Florence Nightingale, Thomas Arnold, General Gordon are pushed one by one off their pedestals. So much had been blasted away, that there was almost a resentment that any should be left standing. 'The thin, angular woman, with her haughty eye and her acrid mouth, had vanished; and in her place was the rounded bulky form of a fat old lady, smiling all day long.' So the holy cardinal becomes the shrewd operator, the earnest enthusiast for Christian education becomes the founder of a cult of athleticism and good form, the pious general becomes a hard drinker. So the old world became a bubble to be pricked, and Strachey, who was at least stylish, was followed by others whose creed was defamation for defamation's sake.

Many of the most famous prose commentaries on the war fell into the period between the two world wars. This was natural, for those in the heat of battle, or even just waiting in dug-outs, do not have the tranquillity or, for the most part, the opportunity to produce such extended reflections. Henri Barbusse was unusual in producing *Le*

Feu while the fighting was still on. But what followed was a product of *l'entre-deux-guerres* as much as of the war itself: on the one hand the sense that civilian life, with the shadow of unemployment and the total absence of homes fit for heroes to live in, was dull and humdrum compared with the adventure and danger of war, and indeed that the rat-race, as we call it to-day, was a poor substitute for the comradeship of the trenches (for one theologian, Charles Raven, later to become a pacifist, that comradeship remained the most inspiring and formative experience of his life); on the other hand, the monumental futility of war, and the hope in the League of Nations, and the desperate attempt to stir the conscience. The first produced *Bull-Dog Drummond*; it is significant that 'Sapper' retained his *nom-de-guerre*. It also produced Flying-Officer W. E. Johns's original Biggles stories in *The Modern Boy*, an authentic account, though much oversimplified, of the war in the air. The Biggles saga tailed off into a series of pot-boilers, but 'The White Fokker', and the stories which immediately followed, were vivid and imaginative. Of course it is schoolboyish, but many, very many, of those who fought were schoolboys, and there was something touchingly schoolboyish about the way they went. This sense of war as romantic adventure was, despite Churchill, almost totally lacking in World War II; it is the reason why Snoopy has to go back to World War I to encounter the Red Baron. At the same time, from all countries came the stream of more or less fictionalized reminiscences turning the readers against war. The most famous was Erich Maria Remarque's *Im Westen nichts Neues (All Quiet on the Western Front)*. Another book from Germany which had a similar effect against the intention of the author was Ernst Jünger's *In Stahlgewittern (The Storm of Steel)*. This appeared in English with a puzzled introduction by an eminent man of letters, who could not understand how the book could read exactly like an Englishman's reminiscences except that Jünger wrote 'British' for 'German', and 'German' for 'British'.

Many of these works, whether autobiographical or fictionalized, appeared in English, first in small numbers, then in a spate ten or twelve years after the armistice, continuing again in a trickle. There was Herbert Read's *In Retreat*, written in 1919 with an artist's eye for detail in a kind of Imagist prose, and published much later. There was C. E. Montague's *Disenchantment, Fiery Particles* and *Rough Justice*; they reflect disenchantment indeed: he endorses a German view of the New Army, 'lions led by donkeys'. There was Mottram's *Spanish Farm* trilogy, a subtle evocation of the social attitudes within the British Army, at its weakest in its battle-scenes, but outstandingly readable. There was Blunden's *Undertones of War*, selectively autobiographical, the product of his continuing preoccupation with the past, keenly observed, underwritten, but shot through and through with the contrast between nature's harmonies and the discord of war. There were Sassoon's semi-autobiographical accounts of George Sherston and his progress, made historical in his later account of his own journey. There was Aldington's pacifist novel *Death of a Hero*, over-earnest, over-didactic, yet powerfully realistic in its account of the actual fighting and the sheer waste of human life. There was H. M. Tomlinson's *All our Yesterdays,* undramatic, indifferently organized, yet sensitive in its description of scenes and people. There was the Australian Frederic Manning's *Her Privates We* with its sense of war as a sexual aberration: an unexpurgated private edition was published under the title, *The Middle Parts of Fortune*. Arnold Bennett said of this that 'it depends for its moral magic on a continuous veracity, consistent, comprehending, merciful and lovely'. Manning called war 'a peculiarly human activity', not just a crime but the punishment of a crime. There was, of course, Wyndham Lewis's *Blasting and Bombadiering*. Perhaps the best of all the autobiographical writing was Graves's *Goodbye to All That*. This book covers a wider canvas than the war, but the war is central to it. It is much more effective than his war poems. It gives an impression of an almost clinical detachment, not least in the account of his own escape from death (he was in fact given up), and his observation of the bubbles of blood coming from his lung-wound. Graves does not glorify or condemn: he describes with close realism and keen analytical observation of himself and others.

A third group of novels do not see the war either as an adventure or as a crime, but as a backcloth to human endeavour. Probably the best of these is Ford Madox Ford's tetralogy about Christopher Tietjens, *Parade's End*. Tietjens is a solid, integral man of the Tory landowning class caught up in the dissolution of a way of life. The war is a part of that break-up, but the corruption runs deeper. The interaction of public and personal is handled with particular brilliance, and the impressionist style fixes moment after moment in the memory. Another work which created an impression in its day was Charles Morgan's *The Fountain*. Morgan (1894–1958) is un-fashionable, a carry-over from a vanished age, though his novels have had a high reputation in France. But he has keen observation, and a limpid style which he learned from George Moore. His major books explore the interaction of love, death and one of the arts. War was an obviously suitable stage for such a theme. In *The Fountain* (1932) the art is the contemplative life, and an internment situation gives ample room for its development. The book contains a strong element of reminiscence, since Morgan, serving with the Naval Brigade of the RNVR, had been interned in Holland after the fall of Antwerp, but had been released on parole and put under the care and protection of a cultured family named de Pallandt on the estate of Rosendaal Castle.

Reminiscences of the war were legion, but for the most part of no literary significance. There was one notable exception, T. E. Lawrence's *Seven Pillars of Wisdom*. The book had a strange career. He wrote it in 1919, lost it at Reading Station, rewrote it from memory in 1920, and then in 1921–2 undertook the final draft. But he was insistent that it should not receive general publication in his lifetime. He did, however, issue a limited edition, superbly printed and illustrated, in 1926, which he paid for by an abridged, popular version entitled *Revolt in the Desert*. The book itself was not generally available till after his death in 1935. His adventures, operating among the Arabs from a base in the intelligence service in Egypt, remain among the most exciting of true war-stories: there was little romance in the mud of Flanders, but romance enough in the sands of Arabia. He tells his story in a clear, workmanlike style derived from C. M. Doughty's *Travels in Arabia Deserta*. His writing has the ease born of great pains. 'Words get richer every time they are deliberately used . . . but only when deliberately used.' He found, he said, his inmost self in writing. It is compulsive reading. Where is there a finer beginning than this?—

Some of the evil of my tale may have been inherent in our circumstances. For years we lived anyhow with one another in the naked desert, under the indifferent heaven.

Mostly he likes an abrupt directness. Chapters begin: 'Lewis and Stokes had come down to help me.' 'Starting was as difficult as ever.' 'I went away north, scouting with Awad.' Sometimes he allows himself the telling adjective or adverb: 'Notwithstanding, these plans quickly went adrift.' 'Quiveringly a citizen woke me.' There are, as we know, reticences in his narrative. A. J. P. Taylor somewhat unkindly said that Lawrence's writing 'provided the upper classes with a substitute for literature'. But no book so persuasively conveys the character of the Arab and the life of the desert.

Edmund Blunden, as has been argued, felt the full power and horror of the war only after it was over. Sassoon said that Blunden remained the poet most obsessed by war. His volumes of *Poems 1914-30* actually contained a section 'War: Impacts and Delayed Actions', and *Undertones of War* appeared ten years after the Armistice. His nature was now red in tooth and claw; witness in 'The Pike':

> While in the shallow some doomed bulrush swings
> At whose hid root the diver vole's teeth gnash.

The beauty seems treacherous. So in 'The Sunlit Vale':

> And never have I seen such a bright bewildering green,
> But it looked like a lie,
> Like a kindly meant lie.

The war haunted him. In 1921 he was writing ('War's People'):

> These after -pieces will not now dispel
> The scene and action, that was learned in hell.

'1916 Seen from 1921' is one of the most remarkable poems in its introspective honesty and in the technical skill with which the heaviness on the heart is conveyed.

> Tired with dull grief, grown old before my day,
> I sit in solitude and only hear
> Long silent laughters, murmurings of dismay,
> The lost intensities of hope and fear;
> In those old marshes yet the rifles
> and I lie, . . .
> Dead as the men I loved, I wait while life drags
> Its wounded length from these sad streets of war
> Into green places here, that were my own.

It was the mud and blood which had become his own. So, eight years later, he wrote 'Return of the Native: Ypres 1929'. His home was in the trenches and the tragedy, and England at peace was a foreign country to him.

Finale and Aftermath

Herbert Read (1893–1968) did not publish *The End of a War* till 1933. It is an ambitious, philosophical poem, uneven and not wholly successful. He takes a single horrific incident to 'serve as a focus for feelings and sentiments otherwise diffuse'. A wounded German officer calls an English battalion into an ambush; he is killed: subsequently the mutilated body of a young girl is discovered who turns out to have been a spy. The poem starts with the Meditation of the Dying German Officer:

> Ich sterbe . . . Life ebbs with an easy flow
> and I've no anguish now. This failing light
> is the world's light: it dies like a lamp
> flickering for want of oil. When the last jump comes
> and the axe-head blackness slips through flesh
> that welcomes it with open but unquivering lips
> then I shall be one with the Unknown
> this Nothing which Heinrich made his argument
> for God's existence: a concept beyond the mind's reach.
> But why embody the Unknown: why give the God
> anything but essence, intangible, invisible, inert?

It ends with the Meditation of the Waking English Officer as he hears the bells which proclaim the Armistice:

> Now I see, either the world is mechanic force
> and this the last tragic act, portending
> endless hate and blind reversion
> back to the tents and healthy lusts
> of animal men: or we act
> God's purpose in an obscure way.

Read does not judge: 'It is not my business as a poet to condemn war (or, to be more exact, modern warfare).' But the poem suffers from this lack of commitment.

It is at least arguable that the outstanding piece of creative writing in English called out by the 1914–18 war did not appear till 1937. This is the epic prose-poem *In Parenthesis* by the Welsh poet-painter David Jones (b.1895). It is a difficult but rewarding work, with its interaction of down-to-earth details of the life of the private soldier, and Celtic mythology.

Can you see anything, sentry.
Nothing corporal.

(Note the double-meaning)

'01 Ball is it, no.
Yes corporal.
Keep a sharp outlook sentry—it is the most elementary
disciplines—sights at 350
Yes corporal.
300 p'r'aps.
Yes corporal.
Starving as brass monkeys—as the Arctic bear's arse—Diawl!—
starved as Pen Nant Govid, on the confines of hell.
Unwise it is to disturb the sentinel.
Do dogs of Annwn glast this starving air—do they ride the
trajectory zone, between the tangled brake above the leaning walls.
This seventh gate is parked tonight.

The account of the assault in Part 7 is superb, sensitive to the mood of the men, objective in its account of death. James Agate compared *In Parenthesis* to Malory rewritten by Joyce. Its richness lies in its variety of mood, the exposure of fear in all its forms, the occasional bitterness, the persuasive tenderness, and in its layers of meaning, material, mythological and religious. Its attraction lies in its painterly use of words, its effect of line and colour. Its strength lies in its honesty.

The last year of the war saw a renewal of Elgar's gifts as a composer. 1918 produced the *Violin Sonata, String Quartet* and *Piano Quintet*, and 1919, the *Cello Concerto*. Elgar came out of the fire of war tempered and chastened. The old extravagance is gone; there is a new economy of writing, almost a quietude. But lyrical beauty has not disappeared and the slow movement of the *Cello Concerto*, elegiac in mood, is one of his most exquisite creations. The *Sonata* (op.82) was first performed on 21 March 1919 by Landon Ronald and W. H. Reed; it is concise and lucid; in the second movement where a solemn opening and close enfold a theme of dreamy lyricism, we seem to detect the mood of the end of the war, and the finale adds a note of triumph. But this work, good as it is, is not among Elgar's greatest achievements. The *String Quartet* (op.83), on the other hand, is the finest of all his chamber works. It also has an exquisite slow movement. The whole seems redolent of the Sussex countryside and the hope of peace. The *Piano Quintet* (op.84), conceived on a larger scale, is less successful as a whole: still, it is a reminder of this last blossoming of his chamber music. The second subject of the opening movement is typical of Elgar, but not at his best. It is a movement which somehow loses its way. The Adagio is generally considered one of his finest. The final movement contains a long period of almost mystic development leading to a blazing climax.

All the three works of 1918 are conservative harmonically. No longer impelled by a desire to innovate, Elgar rests in mature capacity. The fact that at the end of the war he turned to chamber music is important, because by doing so he inspired its revival in Britain.

It is the *Cello Concerto* (op.85) that remains the supreme musical achievement of the end of the war. The peculiar *timbre* of the cello makes it not the easiest of concerto solo instruments, and Elgar has handled it with great discretion. The singing tone of the cello made it appropriate to convey a reassertion of humanity, and that, after the stress of war, is what this work seems to be. Diana McVeagh wrote well of the work: 'The note of resignation heard in it is new; the sense of valediction is painfully strong, and, as it turned out, prophetic. But if the spirit is haunted by an autumnal sadness, it is the sadness of compassion, not pessimism.' The cello asserts itself right at the beginning of the opening Adagio. The second movement is a Scherzo, busy without gaiety. The slow movement is a minor masterpiece, relatively simple in its harmonic structure, based on a single sighing theme. The solo instrument plays almost throughout. Similarly in the final Allegro the apparent joyfulness soon proves evanescent, and the onward movement is perpetually being checked by slower chromatic cadences. The last note is a magical touch. Cecil Parrott called this 'a work apart, by a lonely man in war-time who sees the artistic criteria have altered irreversibly'. It could prove the most durable of all Elgar's works.

In other classical composers, too, the effects of the War lingered. Two notable examples are Bliss and Bax. Arthur Bliss (1891–1975) had fought in the war. His first published composition dates only from 1918. The war seared deep into his creative being, and it was only with the composition of *Morning Heroes*, a large-scale choral and orchestral work, in 1930, that he really exorcized it from his being. War had become literally a nightmare for him, from which he could free himself only by the therapy of composition. Arnold Bax had been aloof from the war. Yet he was of those who felt that his old style was inadequate to world changes. He gradually put Rachmaninov from him and emerged into a more violent orchestral style.

Frank Bridge (1879–1941) was a musician of considerable talent, a superb player of chamber music, who also stood aloof from the war as a pacifist. During the war itself he produced little of importance. Before the war he had been a writer of hackneyed salon-music: such is *A Sea Idyl* (1905). But the war seared him and deepened his music. His compositional technique changed and after the war he wrote a *Piano Sonata* dedicated to a friend who was killed in action. The mood is harsher, the technique far more sophisticated and mature. By 1929 Walton was actually referring to him as 'a modernist in the making'.

Thomas Beecham had been knighted in 1916. It is remarkable that as the war reached its climax he was already looking to the future. In 1917 he followed Bantock in challenging Birmingham to develop its own orchestra. The lack of a concert hall was a pity. 'Your town hall', he said, 'has architectural merit; but it is one of the last places in the world anybody would wish to sing or play in. Everything is wrong about it except the outside.' He returned in 1918: 'A year has gone by since I addressed you on the subject of an orchestra for Birmingham. And of course, you have done nothing!' Beecham's stimulus had something to do with the founding of the City of Birmingham Orchestra in 1920, though the initiative came from the municipality. Similarly, late in 1918, but before the end of the war, he was declaring his intention in a letter to the Lord Mayor of Manchester to endow the city with an Opera House. The financial disaster he suffered prevented him from fulfilling his offer, but was a sign of his vision for the future. Manchester still awaits its Opera House.

It is ironical that the last period of the war saw public patronage of the arts on a scale unprecedented in history, and that at the time when the outcome of the war was still in the balance, the Government was paying artists to bring back a message of discontent from the men at the front. The man responsible, more than any other, for developing the idea that artists should record the war, without fear or favour, was C. F. G. Masterman. Muirhead Bone, a skilled draughtsman, and an unemotional objective reporter, who neither glorified the war nor debunked it, had been appointed an Official War Artist in 1916. The first of the War Artist Exhibitions was held in 1917. But it was actually as late as March 1918 that the Ministry of Information embarked upon a really big imaginative scheme. They had to overcome resistance in the Treasury, who failed to see the propaganda value of pictures which were likely to be exhibited only after the war was over. Fortunately they won that battle. Collecting the artists was a problem, as Masterman recalled,

We had to hunt the world to find the men we desired. We discovered Henry Lamb as Medical Officer in Palestine, Wyndham Lewis and D. P. Roberts in the Artillery in France, John and Paul Nash serving in the infantry in the battles round Ypres, Stanley Spencer a private (forbidden to sketch) in the hills round Salonika and his brother Gilbert as a Red Cross orderly in a hospital off Sinai.

The result was to produce a record of the artistic response to war without real parallel. The isolated genius of Callot or Goya had been there in the past, and none of these men, fine artists though they were, had quite the stature of Goya. But war was a catalyst for them, and, notably in the case of Nevinson, helped them to rise above themselves. For many of the artists, and particularly for the greatest, Paul Nash, war was an important factor in their later development. Associated with this scheme was the Cabinet decision to form a National War Museum (initially in the Imperial Institute, later moved to Lambeth and renamed the Imperial War Museum). War Museums tend to be depressing places, monuments to destruction, and perpetuating a one-sided view of conflict. These elements exist at Lambeth, but alongside them is a feature seldom found in War Museums: a record of war through the eyes of artists of distinction and imagination. It is arguable that the Imperial War Museum offers a more comprehensive view of British artists of the twentieth century than any other gallery except the Tate.

Wyndham Lewis had joined the Army in 1915, and recorded his impressions in his autobiographical *Blasting and Bombardiering* (1937). Two facts stand out from reading this: first, that he was disillusioned about the war and came to view it as a senseless catastrophe; second, that at the same time he was fascinated by the gigantic guns.

Out of their throats had sprung a dramatic flame, they had roared, they had moved back. You could seem them lighted from their mouths, as they hurled into the air their great projectiles, and sank back as they did it. In the middle of the monotonous percussion, which had never slackened for a moment, the tom-toming of interminable artillery, for miles around, going on in the darkness . . . (p.120).

Wyndham Lewis became an official war artist, and painted two remarkable pictures, *A Battery Position in a Wood* (1918), and *A Battery Shelled* (1919). Both have formal links with Cubism, though the scene comes first, and the formal pattern is directed to conveying that scene and Lewis's highly intellectual response to it. Humanity is depersonalized. In *A Battery Shelled* the central figures are robots; the men on the left are human but aloof, indifferent. One has turned away from the scene, one has his cap over his eyes and is half-asleep, the third is watching with impassive detachment. In the earlier picture the men are emerging from their dug-out like ants from an ant-hill. One has the impression of a kind of fusion of Capek's *The Insect Play* and *RUR*. In this picture, too, Lewis has created a bold effect. To the left stark phallus-like cylinders point to the sky. We think at first that they are the guns. They are not; they are the wood, or all that the war has left of it. Most of the guns are covered and camouflaged, still and sinister. Just one gigantic gun is in action; there is a sense of colossal power, and a sense of inevitability in the ordered ranks of shells. But the picture in the end is ironical. The gun sends its projectiles off to the right while shells from an unseen source are bursting around. To what end? There is a curious stillness about the picture: the churned-up ground is almost more mobile than the men. One thinks of one of Owen's line, 'And nothing happens'.

   Paul Nash (1889–1946) increasingly appears the most permanent British painter of the century. His father was a lawyer, and he and his brother were strictly brought up; they might sketch on a Sunday but not paint a finished picture. Paul spent three miserable years at St. Paul's School, failed to enter the Navy, failed in architecture and banking, and struck out on his own in the world of art. From the first he was sensitive to the unusual and unnatural; he could detect the sinister underneath the innocent. He went to the Slade, but his work gave little foretaste of what was to come, and he seemed foursquare in the tradition of British watercolour landscape artists. The war came, and in August 1914 he joined the Artists' Rifles as a private, but for two-and-a-half years served at home, becoming an officer. Then in 1917 he went to the Ypres front. Suddenly his artistry took on new life. 'The impact upon the imagination of a Paul Nash,' wrote Rothenstein, 'of this vast desolation of tortured country, churned to mud, pitted with shell-craters, the grass scorched and trampled, was of the utmost violence. An artist accustomed to handle nature more arbitrarily, or familiar with her harsher aspects, might have taken the spectacle less hardly, but he, who had treated her with such tender respect, was pierced by a sense of outrage. The man who loved the intricate tracery of elms had now to contemplate the shattered stumps of trees without names.' In moments snatched from duty, he began to sketch. A stupid accident led to his being invalided home with a broken rib. When he went back in November 1917 it was as an Official War Artist. He was there only for a few weeks, but, as he wrote in a letter, he had seen things '. . . that would last me my lifetime as food for paintings and drawings.' It was true: 'The headless trees white and withered, without any leaves, done, dead' were in one form or another to people his later dream-paintings.

Paul Nash wrote to his wife in November 1917:

We all have a vague notion of the terrors of a battle, and can conjure up with the aid of some of the more inspired war correspondents and the pictures in the *Daily Mirror* some vision of a battlefield; but no pen or drawing can convey this country—the normal setting of the battles taking place day and night, month after month. Evil and the incarnate fiend alone can be master of this war, and no glimmer of God's hand is seen anywhere. Sunset and sunrise are blasphemous, they are mockeries to man, only the black rain out of the bruised and swollen clouds all through the bitter black of night is fit atmosphere in such a land. The rain drives on, the stinking mud becomes more evilly yellow, the shell holes fill up with green-white water, the roads and tracks are covered in inches of slime, the black dying trees ooze and sweat and the shells never cease. They alone plunge overhead, tearing away the rotting tree stumps, breaking the plank roads, striking down horses and mules, annihilating, maiming, maddening, they plunge into the grave which is this land; one huge grave, and cast upon it the poor dead. It is unspeakable, godless, hopeless. I am no longer an artist interested and curious, I am a messenger who will bring back word from the men who are fighting to those who want the war to go on for ever. Feeble, inarticulate, will be my message, but it will have a bitter truth, and may it burn their lousy souls.

Nash showed his *Void of War* at the Leicester Galleries in May 1918. The art critic, P. G. Konody, subsequently wrote 'I cannot think of a picture that interprets the whole terrible meaning of war as completely and convincingly as Lieutenant Paul Nash's little oil painting "Void"'. Arnold Bennett analysed the picture sensitively:

Lieutenant Nash has seen the Front simply and largely. He has found the essentials of it—that is to say, disfigurement, danger, desolation, ruin, chaos—and little figures of men creeping devotedly and tragically over the waste. The convention he uses is ruthlessly selective. The wave-like formation of shell-holes, the curves of shell-bursts, the straight lines and sharply defined angles of wooden causeways, decapitated trees, the fangs of obdurate masonry, the weight of heavy skies, the human pawns of battle—these things are repeated again and again, monotonously, endlessly. The artist cannot get away from them. They obsess him; and they obsess him because they are the obsession of trench-life.

Nash had been seeking a style. Now, in a sense, he found it. Before him was chaos; he drank it in, selected from it, distilled it, and conveyed it. Rothenstein's words are just: 'Out of infinite horror he distilled a new poetry.' Consider *Hill 60*, a vast, churned-up rolling scene with no humanity in sight. In the foreground is a shell-hole and an empty dug-out; a great pool of water is surging under the falling of a score of shells. There are strands of barbed wire about, and the technique of the picture suggests that they cover the ground. In the background is the sky with tiny aircraft and tiny bursts of flak, and dark clouds with symbolic sunrays bursting from one of them— the only note of hope in desolation. Or consider *The Ypres Salient at Night*. Here it is the star-shells which arrest our attention with their geometric patterns, and they lead our eye to the row of destroyed trees on the left. Only as we look again are we aware that there are soldiers in the picture, three in the background, and three in the foreground, hunched, immobile, intruders on the awesome devastation which they are helping to cause. One of the most famous of Nash's war pictures, *We are Making a New World*, seems a little forced: the ground is too churned up, the mirage in the background self-conscious, and the title unnecessary: this is a dream-landscape, not rooted in reality, prophetic of Nash's future, not representative of his present.

Other official artists who were not well known before the war included John Nash (b.1893), endowed with less talent than his brother Paul but with a love of landscape which gives his pictures of desolation the greater power; Stanley Spencer's brother Gilbert; the Australian Henry Lamb (1883–1960), an able and witty painter, who learned the value of the bird's-eye view; William Roberts (b.1895), a follower of Wyndham Lewis, who used a broadly cubist technique to convey essential form: in *Signallers*, or *Shell Dump*, or above all *The Gas Chamber* he portrays human beings as mechanical aids to war; the Jewish Bernard Meninsky, remembered for his railway station scenes of troops gathering for departure, and his capacity to fill a canvas and convey the impression of a crowd without using more than four or five figures; Eric Kennington, who painted heroic portraits; Wadsworth, though the war did little to change or advance his art.

It was not only the new artists who were commissioned to do official war pictures. Wilson Steer (1860–1943) had painted *Girls Running: Walberswick Pier* twenty years before the outbreak of war, and was never to produce quite so fine a work again. From 1912 onwards he painted coastal scenes and had painted at Porchester, Harwick and Bosham. One of these was commissioned: *Dover Harbour in War* (1918). It was a congenial task. He had difficulties to overcome: problems of weather, petty restrictions, aesthetic problems of balance. On 25 September 1918 he wrote

I don't quite know when I shall be able to return home, it all depends on how the picture goes, I think after many struggles it is beginning to shape, but ships and boats are very obstinate customers to deal with, and after spending much time and labour in painting one in, one finds one has got it in the wrong place. I am doing the harbour from the end of the Admiralty Pier, looking back to the castle and cliffs, and spend most of my time in the studio now which is more agreeable than sitting out on a three-legged stool and being regarded with suspicion; however they have got accustomed to me now at any rate on the Admiralty Pier, and don't bother me any more.

The result is undoubtedly a harmonious and well-balanced picture. The sky is stormy still but bright. The cliffs are like sleeping bastions. The boats and ships rest at ease facing inwards, except for one busy launch tearing away to the right. It is a contrived picture, and yet an accurate record.

At the beginning of the war David Bomberg (1890–1957) had painted four major canvases in a geometric style. In 1918 he was commissioned to do a War Memorial painting for the Canadian government. It seemed the moment of recognition, but it was the moment of rejection—for his design was not accepted. He became bitter and moved violently away from geometric painting; witness his exquisite representations of Petra in 1924. Bomberg's experience is not atypical; the end of the war marked a movement away from an extreme avant-garde position for many modernists, in France as well as Britain.

Perhaps the oddest artistic experience of the war was that of William Orpen (1879–1931). This immensely talented man was, in a material sense, one of the most successful of all British painters of any age; yet he missed greatness. Like Millais before, he opted (in Rothenstein's words) 'in favour of a mastery that was a mastery without compelling purpose'. Irish by birth, he was none the less closely identified with war. He took a simplistic view of the conflict. For him the war itself was not merely a cause, a crusade, but there was a clearcut contrast between the heroism of the soldiers in the trenches and the profiteering of those left at home; he clothed the one group universally in robes of white, and endowed the others with horns and tails. In the early part of the war he painted some searching portraits of generals. In the last year and a half of the war he was, on and off, an official war artist—on and off, because his picture *The Refugee* caused such offence that he was sent home, and allowed to return only in July 1918, and then, before the end of the war, he fell desperately ill in Amiens. He wrote an account of his life in *An Onlooker in France 1917–1919*. He laboured hard, and an artist so gifted could not fail to leave a fascinating record of precise observation. (It was typical that he had a collection of pressed flowers, the first to bloom on the battlefield of the Somme after the devastation.) But only occasionally he shows a deeper sensitivity, perhaps in *Changing Billets: Picardy* or *Bombing: Night*. What does obtrude is a note of exaggerated sentiment, which also shouts from the third-rate verses he composed:

> No man did more
> Before.
> No love has been
> By this world seen
> Like his, since Christ
> Ascended.

Contrast Woodbine Willie, as Rev. G. A. Studdert-Kennedy was affectionately called. Someone at home had called the British soldiers 'an army of saints'. 'An army of saints?' said Studdert-Kennedy at church parade. 'Eyes right, every man, and look at your neighbour.' The note which sounded in his verses obtruded itself into Orpen's more ambitious paintings, *The Thinker on the Butte de Warlencourt* and *Adam and Eve at Péronne*. It is religiosity not religion.

This tendency appears most clearly in his Peace Conference pictures. The contrast between the safe profiteering civilians, in whom he included the politicians, and 'the riddled corpses round Bapaume' overwhelmed him. He might have painted a masterpiece out of this tension, but he had renounced the capacity for tension. He had been charged with painting a group of Allied civilian and military leaders at Versailles. 'I painted the room and then I grouped the whole thirty-nine, or whatever the number was, in the room. It took me nine months' incessant painting; hard work. And then, you know, I couldn't go on. It all seemed so unimportant, somehow. In spite of all these eminent men, I kept thinking of the soldiers who remain in France for ever . . . so I rubbed all the statesmen and commanders out and painted the picture as you see it—the unknown soldier guarded by his dead comrades.' In the darkened room where the treaty was signed stands a draped coffin, and above it two wraith-like figures based on his sketch made during the war, *Blown up— mad*. The idea did not work: it was too artificially conceived and posed, and the original was made even more incongruous by two cherubs floating in mid-air. It was shown in the Royal Academy and raised a storm of vilification. The Imperial War Museum refused it. Still, the people he offended were the people whom he intended to offend, and he had compensatory letters. 'Your wonderful picture the "Peace Conference" represents *Real Peace* because you are fed up with the mockery of Peace.' 'I felt I should so like to thank you for placing in your beautiful picture instead of living men of renown, the simple parable of sacrifice.' 'I venture the assertion that when the "great ones" are gone and forgotten and their destructive minds, who are even now plotting for war, are in dust, your painting will occupy an honoured place in the very museum from which it is now rejected by the temporary custodians of that museum.' The tragedy is that Orpen, who was in many ways an Establishment figure, had the independence to stand against the Establishment, and the skill to do just what he wanted in paint, but his vision was insufficiently penetrating. In a curious way his more orthodox pictures of the Peace Conference express his point more powerfully. The statesmen are dwarfed by the halls in which they meet, and appear petty and posturing.

Stanley Spencer (1891–1959) had won a reputation at the Slade; Tonks commented on the combination of a highly original mind with great powers of draughtsmanship. He had painted two remarkable pictures, *The Apple Gatherers* and *The Nativity*. Cookham (the village where he spent most of his life), the Bible and sex were the three motifs of his brush. The war was an escape from the first, offered an apocalyptic vision out of the second, and a substitute for the third. In 1915, when he joined up, he had left unfinished his well-known *Swan Upping*, the occasion when the swans have their wings clipped, a Cookham scene, yet in its own way violent and sexually exciting. He completed this picture after the war.

Spencer enlisted in the RAMC and served for a period at the Beaufort Hospital (a former lunatic asylum) in Bristol. He did some sketches of patients and orderlies which he gave away, but his memory of those days was vivid, and a sketch done in 1921 (now in the Fitzwilliam Museum, Cambridge) recalled scrubbing floors and washing laundry in the hospital. He applied to go overseas and was sent for training to Tweseldown Camp near Farnham. Then he embarked in the London Docks for Salonika, from where he was sent up country in Macedonia. He wrestled with his religious beliefs, suffered acutely from malaria, sketched his fellow soldiers and (from photographs) their loved ones, noted wild geese flying overhead, a rose in the sun, a mountain torrent speeding down over rocks, Greek peasant women doing their washing. A British offensive in April and May proved abortive, the summer was uneventful and Spencer, impatient for action, volunteered for the infantry. He was regarded as eccentric: when he rescued a wounded officer he heard the man whisper to one of his fellows 'Spencer is not a fool; he is a damned good man', which made him wonder what was usually said about him. There is some indication that a request to release him to become a War Artist was turned down. He saw the war out, ending in hospital with a bad bout of malaria.

Little remains of his war sketches but in 1919 he put his memories on paper in a series of sketches and one major oil-painting (now in the Imperial War Museum) showing *Travoys with Wounded Soldiers Arriving at a Dressing Station at Smol, Macedonia*. He insisted that this was not a scene of horror but a scene of redemption, not a war picture but a peace picture. Eight more years passed before he began his masterpiece of the war, the memorial chapel at Burghclere, near Newbury, in Berkshire. The chapel is adorned with keenly observed scenes of the Macedonian campaigns in the context of a mighty resurrection of soldiers and mules in a military cemetery. 'My wish to do the Burghclere Memorial' he was to say 'was in order to redeem and rescue from those war atmospheres the myself which I everywhere saw, both in myself and others.' He turned the transitory into the permanent. On each side wall are four rectangular predellas; above them four arched panels and above these, with a curiously shaped base, a huge fresco. On the left this represents *The Camp at Karasuli*. Below this we see *A Convoy of Wounded Soldiers arriving at Beaufort Hospital Gates; Ablutions at Beaufort; Kit Inspection at Tweseldown; Stand-to, Macedonia*. Below these are *Scrubbing the Floor; Kit-bags; Laundry; Tea Urns*; these last all reminiscences of Beaufort. On the other side the great fresco is of *River bed at Todorova*. The arched panels have four scenes from Macedonia: *Réveillé; Filling Water-bottles; Map-reading; Making a Fire-belt*. The lower panels are all from Beaufort: *Frost-bite; Tea in the Ward; Bed-making* and the amusing *Scrubbing Lockers*. In his original plan he had a *Surgical Operation*, but decided that this would introduce a note of terror which he did not want. His memory for detail seen ten years or more earlier is astonishing; it is evidenced in his letters as well as in the paintings. The spiritual exaltation with which he portrays ordinary soldiers doing ordinary things makes one think of Sassoon's 'Everyone suddenly burst out singing'. On the end wall is the *Resurrection*. This was a theme which was haunting him at the outset of the War. In 1924–6 he had painted *The Resurrection in Cookham Churchyard*. Now he brought together his religious insight and his war experience. The scene is Kalinova in Macedonia. His first idea was for a pattern of crosses and mules surrounded by a band of vegetation, and he toyed for a long time with using barbed wire as a monstrous, universal crown of thorns. The mules and crosses remain, but among the crosses are recognizable soldiers individually conceived, and in the middle distance. Christ is receiving them. Spencer wanted here to convey the sense of 'coming home'; he found a domesticity in Macedonia which made the longing for home more acute. The neglect of this great work is hard to understand: it should be a major shrine of artistic pilgrimage, and is assuredly the greatest work of English art inspired by the war.

The period of reconstruction after the war should have been a time of major opportunity for artists and architects. Thousands and thousands of war memorials went up all over the country but it is hard to recall a single one of any real distinction. Architecturally, after a period of standstill there was a surge forward in public building but the architects, like the sculptors, failed to grasp the moment, and it was not until the end of the 1920s that buildings fitted to the new age began to emerge from London Transport. The truth is that the British were living in the past; they were still hankering after the world before the war, but that world had gone.

One major project—a Hall of Remembrance, to be adorned with paintings by the major war artists—was planned. The hall itself was eventually shelved but the pictures remain. The centrepiece was to have been Sargent's *Gassed*, an immensely skilful picture of a grim procession of soldiers with their eyes bandaged; it is full of pathos which goes far beyond the injured individuals, for there is an overwhelming sense of a world in which the blind are leading the blind. George Clausen's picture *In the Gun Factory at Woolwich Arsenal* has become little more than a darkly pleasant picture; all urgency is gone. By contrast, Nevinson produced a stridently obvious *The Harvest of Battle*; the unpeopled mudscapes of 1915-16 are far more eloquent. There were better pictures. Henry Lamb's *Irish Troops in the Judaean Hills Surprised by a Turkish Bombardment* is seen from above, almost with divine compassion. The figures are at all angles, agonized, uncertain, as smoke drifts mystically across the scene. Stanley Spencer was called out too late to record the war, but from earlier sketches contributed to the project his *Travoys with Wounded Soldiers arriving at a Dressing Station, Smol, Macedonia*. Here, too, is the divine view which the development of aircraft must have suggested. We are aware of the mules, of the poles of the stretchers, and only then of the hunched forms under the blankets. And everywhere there are hands, strong in steadying, gentle in helping and healing, contorted in pain. John Nash's *Oppy Wood: Evening* is more contrived than his brother's best work—the arrangement of duckboard or corrugated iron is more artificial—but there is the same sense of desolation, and the same impression that men do not really belong here. The finest of all the paintings for the project is Paul Nash's *The Menin Road*; it sums up in a single large canvas his previous achievement. Here we find a brilliant design, contrived but not artificial. There is strong sexual symbolism. The gaunt trees stand like erect phalluses, the shell-hole in the foreground speaks of the rape of the earth. The tranquil reflections nearby contrast with the violent turbulence of the sky pierced with searchlights. The soldiers, hardly noticeable at first, are alien intruders moving across a scene where they have no right to be. This is, surely, a masterwork.

Jacob Epstein (1880–1959) responded to the war with a statue of *The Risen Christ*. Although he did not exhibit it until 1920, it was begun in 1917. Bernard Van Dieren, the composer, was ill in bed. Epstein went to talk to him. 'Watching his head, so spiritual and worn with suffering, I thought I would like to make a mask of him. I hurried home and returned with clay and made a mask which I immediately recognized as the Christ head, with its short beard, its pitying, accusing eyes, and the lofty and broad brow, denoting great intellectual strength.' It was like the scene in Turgeniev, when the writer suddenly feels in an ordinary man beside him in the crowd, the presence of the Christ. Epstein began to see the whole figure, barefoot, swathed in clothes, pointing with an accusing finger at his wounded hand. The notorious publicist Father Bernard Vaughan rose in wrath: 'I felt ready to cry out with indignation that in this Christian England there should be exhibited the figure of a Christ which suggested to me some degraded Chaldean or African, which wore the appearance of an Asiatic-American or Hun-Jew, which reminded me of some emaciated Hindu, or a badly grown Egyptian swathed in the cerements of the grave.' It would certainly seem that Epstein achieved a Universal Christ! Others looked deeper than Vaughan. John Middleton Murry saw the figure as a Christ-Prometheus, a Christ who has suffered as a man and triumphed as a man. Frank Rutter approved 'a strong, stern, ascetic young Christ'. Rev. Edward Shillito pointed out that this Christ was the fierce and even violent leader of men, stern and austere, and yet terrible in His intensity of passion, and that this was true to one aspect of the Gospel story. And Epstein himself, writing later, put his finger into its historical context.

I must maintain that my statue of Christ still stands for what I intended it to be. It stands and accuses the world for its grossness, inhumanity, cruelty, and beastliness, for the First World War and for the later wars in Abyssinia, China, and Spain which culminated in the Second World War . . . I should like to remodel the 'Christ'. I should like to make it hundreds of feet high, and set it up on some high place where all could see it, and where it would give out its warning, its mighty symbolic warning to all lands. The Jew—the Galilean—condemns our wars, and warns us that 'Shalom, Shalom', must be still the watchword between men and men.

As we look at the world scene few of the significant creative artists were identified with the war. Friedrich Gundolf had declared 'He who has the power to create also had the right to destroy.' Thomas Mann had for a while been of like mind, seeing in the strife German *Kultur* resisting barbarism ('can one be a musician without being German?') and bringing purification, liberation and hope. It was not long before he rejected all such nationalism as illusion. For most it was agony. Another German writer, Walter van Molo, said 'Misery reaches into the soul. Souls that have been scrubbed clean of misery produce a deeper art than well-fed complacency.' Proust, developing *Remembrance of Things Past* in Paris, saw the war as 'a substance interposed between me and all objects. As men once lived in God, so I live in this war.' Some had entered into the war before it began. Paul Klee wrote in his diary: 'I have long had this war in me. Therefore it does not concern me inwardly.' Kokoschka had a prophetic vision of himself in uniform with hand chopped off. The poet Georg Trakl saw the war as a visitation for guilt; 'I do not have the right to withhold myself from Hell.' Franz Werfel wrote pacifist essays, Stefan Zweig an antiwar play. Rilke hated his uniform, and spent the war 'unable to comprehend, unable to comprehend, unable to comprehend.' Too many did not return—Apollinaire and Péguy, and Albéric Magnard, and Boccioni and Franz Marc. Braque and Kokoschka were wounded. Beckmann and Kirchner suffered breakdowns. Kafka began coughing blood: 'The world and I are tearing my body apart in an insoluble conflict.' All the stylistic elements which they used to express their agony and compassion, in sound and paint and words, existed before the war. If there was a movement, it was to emphasize the elements already found in expressionism. The Austrian writer Robert Musil said in 1919: 'Before I went into the war, we had an explosive, intellectually imaginative poetry, a lyric poetry of intellectual intentions. . . . When I returned there was *expressionism*.' The war in Europe was at once an interlude and an intensification.

The war did not create a revolution in the Arts in Britain either. Britain had been insensitive to the global changes before the war, and remained so afterwards. Painters, musicians, writers, for the most part remain impenitently and impenetrably insular. If anything, the isolation of culture in the war years intensified this process. In art and music the war did little to promulgate new styles. It is an interesting experience to walk through the rooms in the Tate which contain British art of the early twentieth century. There is no obvious way of discerning the pre-war from the post-war. The same is true in music. If we consider song, the pastoral tradition which was strong before the war emerged unscathed after the war. Butterworth had taken up Housman's poetry, and *A Shropshire Lad* provided some of the most popular texts for the song-writers of the 1920s. But there was one difference in music. British performers began to come into their own, and British composers to receive more of a hearing, so that the way opened to a great upsurge in British music at all levels.

The really significant change was in poetry. The poets, whether soldier or civilian, found the old modes inadequate to the experience of heroic but futile destruction and to the empty conventionality of the old order. In their different ways Owen and Eliot created a new poetry, Owen through the modification of old forms, Eliot through the control of the new. The biggest impact of the war on the Arts was indirect. It was the explosion which brought down the cracked fabric of the old society. Yeats saw it in 1919:

> Many ingenious lovely things are gone
> That seemed sheer miracle to the multitude,
> Protected from the circle of the moon
> That pitches common things about. There stood
> Amid the ornamental bronze and stone
> An ancient image made of olive wood—
> And gone are Phidias' famous ivories
> And all the golden grasshoppers and bees.

And, more familiarly:

> Surely some revelation is at hand;
> Surely the Second Coming is at hand.
> The Second Coming! Hardly are those words out

115

When a vast image out of *Spiritus Mundi*
Troubles my sight: somewhere in sands of the desert
A shape with lion body and the head of a man,
A gaze blank and pitiless as the sun,
Is moving its slow thighs, while all about it
Reel shadows of the indignant desert birds.
The darkness drops again; but now I know
That twenty centuries of stony sleep
Were vexed to nightmare by a rocking cradle.
And what rough beast, its hour come round at last,
Slouches towards Bethlehem to be born?

Bibliography, Mainly of Secondary Material

Anon (ed)   *Poems of the Great War*   (London 1914)

Baily, L.   *BBC Scrapbooks* vol I 1896–1914   (London 1966)

Bairnsfather, B.   *The Bystander's Fragments from France*   (London n.d.)

Baynes, K.   *War*   (London 1970)

Beal, A.   *D. H. Lawrence*   (London 1961)

Bennett, A.   *Journals* ed. N. Flower   (London 1932–3)

Bentley, E.   *Bernard Shaw*   (London 1967)

Bergonzi, B.   *Heroes' Twilight: A Study of the Literature of the Great War*   (London 1965)

Beaver, P. (ed)   *The Wipers Times*   (London 1973)

Beecham, Sir Thomas   *A Mingled Chime*   (London 1948)

Bell, Q.   *Bloomsbury*   (London 1968)

Berry, W. H.   *Forty Years in the Limelight*   (London 1939)

Bertram, A.   *Paul Nash: The Portrait of an Artist*   (London 1958)

Bertram, A.   *Paul Nash*   (London 1923)

Bertram, A.   *Augustus John*   (London 1923)

Bertram, A.   *A Century of British Painting 1851–1951*   (London 1951)

Blunden, E. (ed.)   *The Poems of Wilfred Owen*   (London 1963)

Blunden, E.   *War Poets 1914–1918*   (London 1958)

Carline, R.   *Stanley Spencer at War*   (London 1978)

Cassell, R. A.   *Ford Madox Ford: A Study of his Novels*   (Baltimore 1961)

Chapple, J. A. V.   *Documentary and Imaginative Literature 1880–1920*   (London 1970)

Clarke, C. (ed)   *D. H. Lawrence: The Rainbow and Women in Love*   (London 1969)

Cooke, W.   *Edward Thomas: A Critical Biography*   (London 1970)

Clarke, G. H. (ed)   *A Treasury of War Poetry*   (London 1917)

Colles, H. C.   *Walford Davies: A Biography*   (London 1942)

Collis, M.   *Stanley Spencer*   (London 1962)

Crompton, L.   *Shaw the Dramatist*   (London 1971)

Dangerfield, G. *The Strange Death of Liberal England 1910–1914* (London 1961)

de Witt, H. *Bawdy Barrack-Room Ballads* (London 1970)

Davies, Walford Letter to *The Times* (27.8.1927)

Dodgson, C. and Montague, C. F. *British Artists of the Front* (London 1918)

Ellman, Richard *James Joyce* (New York 1959)

Edmonds, C. *A Subaltern's War* (London 1929)

Epstein, J. *An Autobiography* (London 1955)

Ferguson, J. (ed) *War and the Creative Arts* (London 1972)

Ferguson, J. 'Art in Two World Wars' in *War, The Arts, and Ideas* Open University A301 *Block IX Units 24–6* (Milton Keynes 1973)

Ford, B. (ed) *The Modern Age* (Pelican Guide to English Literature 7) (Harmondsworth 1967)

Forster, E. M. *Goldsworthy Lowes Dickinson* (London 1934)

Gaisberg, F. *Music on Record* (London 1946)

Gardner, B. *Up the Line to Death: The War Poets 1914–1918* (London 1964)

Gaunt, W. *The March of the Moderns* (London 1949)

Geduld, H. M. *James Barrie* (New York 1971)

Golding, D. *Reputations* (London 1920)

Graves, C. L. *Hubert Parry* 2 vols. (London 1926)

Graves, R. *Good-bye to all that* (London 1929)

Grunfeld, F. V. *The Story of Great Music: The Early Twentieth Century* (New York ND)

Hassall, C. *Rupert Brooke* (London 1964)

Holst, I. *The Music of Gustav Holst* (London 1968)

Hubbard, H. *A Hundred Years of British Painting 1951–1951* (London 1951)

Hudson, D. *James Pryde* (London 1949)

Hussey, M. (ed) *Poetry of the First World War* (London 1967)

Hergestein, H. *Hugh Walpole: An Appreciation* (New York 1919)

Hoffman, C. G. *Ford Madox Ford* (New York 1967)

Johnston, J. H. *English Poetry of the First World War: A Study in the Evolution of Lyric and Narrative Form* (Princeton 1964)

Johnstone, J. K. *The Bloomsbury Group* (New York 1963)

Jones, D. *In Parenthesis* (London 1937)

Kennedy, M. *The Hallé Tradition* (Manchester 1960)

Kenner, H. *The Poetry of Ezra Pound* (London 1951)

Konody, P. G. and Dark, S. *Sir William Orpen* (London 1932)

Leavis, F. R. *D. H. Lawrence, Novelist* (London 1955)

Lewis, P. Wyndham *Blasting and Bombardiering* (London 1967)

Bibliography

Liddell Hart, B. H.   *History of the First World War*   (London 1970)
MacDonagh, M.   *In London during the Great War*   (London 1935)
Mackerness, E. G.   *A Social History of English Music*   (London 1964)
Mackenzie-Rogan, J.   *Fifty Years of Army Music*   (London 1926)
Marrot, M. V.   *The Life and letters of John Galsworthy*   (London 1935)
Martin, G.   *D. H. Lawrence's The Rainbow* (Open University A100 Units 35–6)   (Milton Keynes 1971)
Marwick, A.   *The Deluge: British Society and the First World War*   (London 1965)
Marwick, A.   *War and Social Change in the Twentieth Century*   (London 1974)
Masterman, L.   *C. F. G. Masterman*   (London 1939)
Maxwell, W. B.   *Time Gathered*   (London 1937)
McVeagh, D.   *Edward Elgar: His Life and Music*   (London 1955)
Meixner, J. A.   *Ford Madox Ford's Novels*   (Minneapolis 1962)
Montague, C. E.   *The Front Line*   (London 1917)
Montague C. E.   *Disenchantment*   (London 1922)
Montague, C. E.   *Rough Justice*   (London 1926)
Moore, H. T.   *The Intelligent Heart*   (Harmondsworth 1960)
Morgan, M. M.   *The Shavian Playground*   (London 1972)
Nash, P.   *Outline: An Autobiography: and other writings*   (London 1949)
Nevinson, C. R. W.   *Modern War*   (London 1917)
Nevinson, C. R. W.   *Paint and Prejudice*   (London 1937)
Nevinson, C. R. W.   *The Great War: fourth year*   (London 1918)
Nichols, R.   *Anthology of War Poetry 1914–18*   (London 1943)
Orpen, W.   *An Onlooker in France 1917–1919*   (London 1924)
Owen, H.   *Journey from Obscurity: Wilfred Owen 1893–1918*   (London 1963–5)
Owen, H. and Bell, J. (ed)   *Collected Letters of Wilfred Owen*   (London 1967)
O'Byrne, Dermot   *A Dublin Ballad and other poems*   (Dublin 1918)
Paige, D. D. (ed)   *The Letters of Ezra Pound 1907–1941*   (London 1961)
Parrott, I.   *Elgar*   (London 1971)
Pinto, V. de S.   *Crisis in English Poetry 1880–1940)*   (London 1951)
Porter, J. F.   *Sir Edward Elgar*   (London 1921)
Porteous, H. G.   *Wyndham Lewis*   (London 1932)
Press, J. B.   *A Map of Modern English Verse*   (London 1969)
Raknan, I.   *H. G. Wells and His Critics*   (Oslo and London 1962)
Read, H.   *In Retreat*   (London 1925)
Read, H.   *Annals of Innocence and Experience*   (London 1940)
Reid, C.   *Thomas Beecham*   (London 1967)
Richards, F.   *Old Soldiers Never Die*   (London 1933)

Roberts, M. *The Faber Book of Modern Verse* (London 1936)

Robinson, W. Heath *Some Frightful War Pictures* (London n.d.)

Rosenbaum, S. P. (ed) *The Bloomsbury Group* (London 1975)

Rosenberg, I. *Collected Works* (London 1937)

Rothenstein, J. *British Artists and the War* (London 1931)

Rothenstein, J. *Modern English Painters* 2 vols. (London 1952)

Rowland, Kurt A. *A History of the Modern Movement: Art Architecture Design* (London 1973)

Sager, K. *The Art of D. H. Lawrence* (Cambridge 1966)

Sassoon, S. *Memories of an Infantry Officer* (London 1930)

Sassoon, S. *Siegfried's Journey 1916–20* (London 1945)

Scott-Sutherland, C. *Arnold Bax* (London 1973)

Searle, H. and Layton R. *Twentieth Century Composers III Britain, Scandinavia and the Netherlands* (London 1972)

Shaw, G. B. *Heartbreak House* (London 1919)

Shaw, G. B. *What I really wrote about the War* (London 1930)

Silkin, J. *Out of Battle: The Poetry of the Great War* (London 1972)

Stallworthy, J. *Wilfred Owen* (London 1974)

Stallworthy, J. *Poets of the First World War* (London 1974)

Stead, C. K. *The New Poetic: Yeats to Eliot* (Harmondsworth 1967)

Strachey, L. *Eminent Victorians* (London 1918)

Swinnerton, F. *The Georgian Literary Scene* (London 1935)

Taylor, A. J. P. *English History 1914–45* (Oxford 1965)

Tomlinson, H. M. *All Our Yesterdays* (London 1930)

Trewis, S. C. *Benson and the Bensonians* (London 1960)

Ward, M. *Gilbert Keith Chesterton* (London 1944)

Wees, W. C. *Vorticism and the English Avant-Garde* (Manchester 1972)

Weintrant, S. *Journey to Heartbreak: The Crucible Years of Bernard Shaw 1914–1918* (New York 1971)

Wiley, P. L. *Novelist of Three Worlds: Ford Madox Ford* (Syracuse 1962)

Williams, M. 'Literature and the First World War' in *World War I* (Open University A301 Block V Units 14–17) pp. 153–80 (Milton Keynes 1973)

Williamson, H. *A Soldier's Diary of the Great War* (London 1929)

Welland, D. 'Arthur Graeme West: A Messenger to Job' in Hibbard, G. R. (ed) *Renaissance and Modern Essays: Presented to V de Sola Pinto* (London 1966)

Woolf, V. *Roger Fry: A Biography* (London 1940)

Bibliography

Files of

ARTS COUNCIL EXHIBITION CATALOGUES
BLAST
BURLINGTON MAGAZINE
CONNOISSEUR
EGOIST
ILLUSTRATED LONDON NEWS
MORNING POST
MUSICAL QUARTERLY
MUSICAL TIMES
MUSIC AND LETTERS
NEW AGE
NEW WITNESS
PENROSE'S ANNUAL
ROYAL ACADEMY ILLUSTRATED
TIMES
TIMES LITERARY SUPPLEMENT

Index

Index

Marne 15, 26
Masefield, John 8, 55–6
Marsh, Edward 4, 19, 47, 89
Martyn, Edward 4
Marwick, A. x, 70
Mason, A. E. W. 51
Mason, J. H. 29
Masterman, C. F. G. 102–3
Matisse, H. 9
Maxwell, W. B. 51
McCarthy, Lillah 8
McEwen, J. B. 24
McNeile, Cyril *see* 'Sapper'
McVeagh, Diana 101
mechanization 30, 73–4, 107
Mendelssohn, F. 1
Mendl, R. W. S. 64
Meninsky, Bernard 107
Meredith, G. 4
Mesopotamia 16, 52
militarism, debasing effects of 24
Milne, A. A. 51
Mlynarski, Emil 24
Modern Boy, The 95
monologue, dramatic 57
monosyllables 88, 89
Montague, C. E. 95–6
Morgan, Charles 96–7
Moore, George 5, 50–1, 97
Morrell, Lady Ottoline 6
—, Philip 6
Morris, William 2
Mottram, R. H. 96
Murray, Gilbert 8, 31
Murry, J. M. 113
music 1, 3, 6–7, 22–5, 56–66, 76, 100–2, 115
—, cinema 63
music-halls 57, 62
Music in Wartime Committee 23
Musical Standard, The 25
Musical Times, The 22
mythology 5

Nash, John 103, 107, 112
Nash, Paul 73, 74, 103, 104–6, 113
Nation, The 70
National Gallery 1, 70
National Portrait Gallery 1
nationalism 4, 114
—in music 23, 63

navy-life 54
Nevinson, C. R. W. 11, 12, 26, 73–4, 103, 112
Newbolt, Henry 17–18,
New Statesmen, The 31, 70
New Witness, The 91
Nicholls, Agnes 59
Nichols, Robert 41–2
Nicholson, Ben 71
No-Conscription Fellowship 31
novelists 4, 34–9, 96–7
Novello, Ivor 64

Observer, The 70
O'Byrne, Dermot 76
O'Grady, Standish 4
Omega workshops 29, 72
O'Neill, Norman 24
Onions, Oliver 51–2
opera 7, 23
Oppenheim, E. Phillips 53
opponents of war 31–2
optimism 3
orchestras 7, 22–4, 62, 63
Orpen, William 71, 108–10
Owen, Wilfred 46, 84–8, 91, 104, 115
Oxenham, John 17

pacifism 6, 28–9, 81, 94, 95, 96, 102
Pain, Barry 52
painting 3, 9–11, 12–14, 27, 71–4, 102–13
Pall Mall Gazette, The 89
parody 65–6, 67, 74
Parrott, Cecil 101
Parry, Hubert 24, 58, 60
patriotism 16–17, 26, 43, 53, 57, 87
Peace Conference 109–10
Peach, Harry 29
Pearse, Padraic 76–7
Pearson, Hesketh 93
Pennell, Joseph 29
Penrose's Annual 30
photography 74–5
Picasso, Pablo 3, 9, 13, 89
Pinero, A. W. 7–8
Pinto, V. da Sola 20
Pissarro, Lucien 71–2
Pitt, Percy 24
poetry 3, 4, 11–12, 17–22, 41–7, 48–50, 81–91, 98–100

129

Index

Somme 24, 40, 44, 56, 79
songs, marching 64
—, pastoral 115
—, popular 65–6
—, recruiting 62
Sorel, G., *Reflections on Violence* 12
Sorley, Charles Hamilton 21–2
speech-rhythms 4, 11
Spencer, Gilbert 103, 107
Spencer, Stanley 10, 103, 110–12
spy-stories 53, 55
Squire, J. C. 18
stagecraft 9
Stainer, J. 1
Stanford, C. V. 7, 23, 24
Steer, P. Wilson 107
Stephens, James 6
Stock, Ralph 52
Strachey, Lytton 6, 94
Strauss, Richard 7
Stravinsky, I. 3, 6–7
Studdert-Kennedy, Revd. G. A. 109
Swayne, Martin 52
Swinburne, A. C. 4, 8
symbolism 47, 51, 73, 77, 113
Synge, J. M. 4

Tate Gallery 1, 103, 115
Taylor, A. J. P. 40, 98
Tchekhov, A. 69
Temple Smith, Hamilton 29
Tennant, E. W. 89
Tennyson, A. 3
Terriss, Ellaline 8
textiles 2, 29
theatre in wartime 25–6, 62, 68–9
—, new development in 9
—, sense of 4, 69
Theatre *see* Abbey, Court, Her Majesty's, Lyceum, Savoy
Thomas, Beach 67
Thomas, Edward 43
Thorndike, Sybil 68
Tilley, Vesta 62
Times, The 10, 19, 20, 51, 92
Tomlinson, H. M. 96
Tonks, Henry 110
Tree, Herbert 8
trench-life 53–4, 67–8, 95
Trewin, J. C. 68
troops, entertainment of 62–6

Turner, W. J. 64

Utopia 51

Vanbrugh, Irene 8

Van Dieren, Bernard 113
Van Gogh, V. 9
Vaughan, Fr. Bernard 113
Vaughan Williams, R. 24, 60–1
Vedrenne, J. E. 9
Vernède, R. E. 18, 52
Vorticists 12–14, 27, 75
Voysey, Charles Annersley 2
Vrogden, Gwendoline 62

Wadsworth, Edward 71, 107
Wagner, R. 23, 24–5
Wallace, Edgar 53
Wallace, William 24
Wallace Collection 1
Walpole, Hugh 35–6
Walton, William 102
War Artist, Official 102–8
War, Boer 5, 16, 20
—, Franco-Prussian 21
— Memorials 108, 112
— that will end War 33
—, World, events of 15–16, 40–1, 79–80
Watson, William 18
Wehrmacht 4
Wells, H. G. 4, 33, 47–8, 92–3
West, A. G. 42–3
Wheels 88–9
Whistler, J. M. 2, 10–11
Whitehead, A. N. 31
Whitworth Institute 1
Wilde, Oscar 8, 11
Williams, Merryn 19
Wipers Times, The 67–8
Witt, R. E. 26
women, participation by 41, 62
Wood, Henry 7, 24, 57, 62
Woodbine Willie *see* Studdert-Kennedy
Woolf, Virginia 6
Wright brothers 4
Wyllie, W. L. 27

Yeats, W. B. 4–5, 6, 9, 72, 115–16
Ypres 15, 40, 44, 74, 98, 103, 105, 106

131